EMPRESS TO THE ORIENT

by W. Kaye Lamb

George Stephen, first President of Canadian Pacific wrote, in 1885, that the railway would not be complete "until we have an ocean connection with Japan and China."

Vancouver Maritime Museum, 1991.

All rights reserved. No part of this book may be reproduced in any form or by any means without written permission from the publisher.

Copyright by the Vancouver Maritime Museum Society 1991.

Published by the Vancouver Maritime Museum Society.
1905 Ogden Avenue, Vancouver, B.C. V6J 1A3.

ISBN -0-9695221-2-6

Printed in Canada.

DEDICATION

While it would hardly be considered proper form for an author to inscribe him- or herself as dedicatee, the publisher, however, has no qualms about dedicating the whole of this book to

**Dr. W. Kaye Lamb
and to
Omer Lavallée and Robert D. Turner
and to
Dr. Wallace B. Chung**

all historians and collectors, for their exemplary work in securing, preserving and presenting the history of the Canadian Pacific Railway Company as a major factor in the record of Canada — and doing it with so much authoritativeness, style and enjoyment.

ACKNOWLEDGEMENTS

The original three essays by W. Kaye Lamb which form the core of this book were published in the British Columbia Historical Quarterly under the following titles and in the following issues:

"The Pioneer Days of the Trans-Pacific Service: 1887-1891" in B.C.H.Q., Vol. I, No. 3.
"Empress to the Orient" in B.C.H.Q., Vol. IV, nos. 1 & 2.
"Empress Odyssey: A History of the Canadian Pacific Service to the Orient, 1913-45" in B.C.H.Q., Vol. XII, no. 1.

Copyright to all the contents of the British Columbia Historical Quarterly is held by the British Columbia Archives and Record Service. The Service, through the Provincial Archivist, Mr. John A. Bovey, has very kindly given its consent to the reprinting of the text in this modified form, the modifications having been undertaken by the original author, Dr. W. Kaye Lamb.

****

The production of this volume has been supported, in part, by

Canadian Pacific Limited and Dr. Wallace B. Chung

****

Design and lay-out, including cover	Gary Tucker
Illustrations selection	Leonard G. McCann and Gary Tucker
Format and lay-out	John Grey-Noble, Umbrella Graphics
Printing	Blok Printing
Photography	B.C. Photographics
	P.S. Photography
	Henry Tabbers
Typing	Beverly Pinnegar

Contents

Foreward   by Leonard G. McCann   **6.**

The Pioneer Days of the Trans - Pacific Service   **7.**

Empress to The Orient   **33.**

Empress Odyssey   **76.**

Footnotes   **131.**

Appendices   **138.**

Catalogue of Illustrations   **148.**

FOREWORD

At Craigellachie in Eagle Pass in the mountains east of Revelstoke, B.C. a spike was hammered home in a rail at 9:22 a.m. on November 7, 1885. The railway link across Canada was now complete — in fulfilment of the terms that brought British Columbia into the Canadian Confederation on July 20, 1871. The Canadian Pacific Railway Company, the proprietors of that link, would now be able to enlarge on the plans for a transportation and communications service across Canada, a service that would ultimately span the globe.

The story presented here is that of one of the other links in that transportation service, this being the marine link between Canada's West Coast and the Orient. At the outset the link was established by means of a number of chartered ships, both sail and steam, and was continued and concluded with a fleet of purpose-built liner/freighters whose colloquial designation of 'White Empresses' underscored the standard, both personal and commercial, that was set by these ships.

Three essays were published in sundry issues of the British Columbia Historical Quarterly between the years of 1937 and 1948. They covered the record of the C.P.R.'s trans-Pacific service from sailing ships to turbine steamers. They were written by W. Kaye Lamb when he was first Provincial Archivist and Librarian and later Librarian of the University of British Columbia. For many years they constituted the sole and authorative record of the operations of the White Empresses.

In 1991, the Vancouver Maritime Museum mounted an exhibition entitled "Empress to the Orient" to mark the centenary of the start of the trans-Pacific Service of the White Empresses of the C.P.R. from Vancouver and Victoria to ports in the Orient. A text to accompany the exhibition was sought. Dr. Lamb, now retired Dominion Archivist and Librarian of Canada, very kindly agreed to review his original essays as the possible text. New material was added, the structure of some of the content was changed so as to reflect post-war realities, a postscript was included which updated the final record and a quantity of illustrations, many never before made available in publication form, also was added; all have provided a new dimension to the story of the fleet of the White Empresses.

The history of the Canadian Pacific Railway Company can be found in considerable detail elsewhere, in many forms and publications. This aspect of its corporate life is, however, unique in that it bears on its maritime operations on Canada's West Coast and is based on original sources. Dr. Lamb's personal knowledge and association with the men, women and ships of the fleet extends back to those who were participants in the establishment of the service. Thus, this long out-of-print and unavailable record, now thoroughly revised and illustrated, is presented as the core for the Vancouver Maritime Museum's centenary salute to the White Empresses of the Pacific.

Leonard G. McCann
Curator
Vancouver Maritime Museum

Vancouver, B.C.
September, 1991

THE PIONEER DAYS OF THE TRANS - PACIFIC SERVICE 1887 - 1891

Parthia: discharging cargo, Vancouver, 1887.

A steamship line from its Pacific terminus to the Orient was from the first an essential part of the plan for a Canadian transcontinental railway. The attractions of the scheme were partly military; and the lively interest taken by the British Government in the railway was due largely to the fact that, in conjunction with steamers on the Atlantic and the Pacific, it would provide an all-British route to the Orient and Australasia. But commercial considerations entered the picture as well; and it was these that George Stephen, first President of the Canadian Pacific, had in mind when he wrote, in 1885, that the railway would not be complete "until we have an ocean connection with Japan and China." Years before, Stephen's interest in the trade possibilities of the Orient had been roused by James Morrison, a London merchant who had befriended him in early days; and as early as October, 1884, he had journeyed to England with the object of arranging for a steamer service between Port Moody and Japan and China.

Two months later it was reported in the press that he had succeeded in his mission; but the announcement was premature. Nevertheless, the Imperial authorities were genuinely interested; and in October, 1885, a month before the last spike was driven at Craigellachie, the Postmaster-General in Lord Salisbury's administration advertised for tenders for the carriage of mails from Vancouver to Hong Kong. The Canadian Pacific responded with an offer to provide a fortnightly service, maintained by steamers built under the supervision of the Admiralty and capable of an average speed of 13 to 14 knots, for a subsidy of £100,000 per annum.[1] In addition, the Company undertook to carry the mails from Halifax to Vancouver free of charge. The only other tender submitted asked for a higher subsidy for a slower service, but the Canadian Pacific proposal was not accepted. The reason given officially for its rejection was the fact that the subsidy already paid to the Peninsular & Oriental (P. & O.) line for the carriage of mails to China via Suez would not be reduced by the proposed service. Actually, a change in government and the crisis over the Irish Home Rule Bill seem to have played an important part. In any event the Directors of the Railway were by no means discouraged, and reported to the shareholders that their plans fitted in so well with Imperial interests that they were confident "that their proposals must soon be accepted by Her Majesty's Government."[2]

W.B. Flint

Alexander

Meanwhile the Company was not content to let the Oriental trade go by default. Regular transcontinental train service was due to commence between Montreal and Port Moody late in June, 1886, and the Railway was anxious to secure a share of the traffic as soon as its line was in operation. An arrangement was therefore made with Frazar & Company, a well-known importing firm, to act as agents for the Canadian Pacific in Japan and China; and during the last half of 1886 seven sailing ships were chartered and dispatched to Port Moody with cargoes consisting mostly of Japanese tea. The first of these was the now famous American barque *W.B. Flint*, which arrived in the Royal Roads on July 26 and reached Port Moody in tow of the tug *Alexander* the following day. "Her arrival," according to the *Vancouver News*, "created much talk and interest among the citizens," and as she passed up the Inlet they "inspected her closely by the aid of field glasses."[3] Her cargo consisted of 17,430 half-chests of tea totalling 1,240,753 pounds. It was consigned chiefly to Toronto, Hamilton, Chicago, and New York. A special effort was made to handle this first shipment of Oriental goods as rapidly as possible, and the Railway succeeded in breaking all previous transcontinental freight records. Shipments reached Montreal on August 7, 47 days from Yokohama, and New York two days later.[4]

Point Atkinson Light.

W.B. Flint : unloading tea, Port Moody, July 28, 1886.

Flora P. Stafford: unloading tea, Port Moody, August, 1886.

The second vessel to arrive, the *Flora P. Stafford*, reached Port Moody on August 27. She carried 26,918 packages of tea totalling 1,658,074 pounds. Captain Smith, her commander, reported that she had been pursued for several days by Chinese pirates. The third arrival was the small Australian barque *Zoroya*, which sailed up to within a few miles of Point Atkinson lighthouse without the assistance of either a tug or a pilot. The feat was not unusual, but was regarded as important because the contention that the Inlet was difficult of access was still heard in certain quarters. The *Zoroya* tied up at Port Moody on September 17 with 529,206 pounds of tea from Hiogo, Japan. She was followed by the German barque *Bylgia*, Captain Weiss, which arrived on October 12, after a record passage of only 22 1/2 days from Yokohama to Cape Flattery. She, too, was a small vessel and her tea cargo totalled about 550,000 pounds. The remaining three ships of this pioneer tea fleet were larger craft. The *Carrie Delap*, which reached the Royal Roads on October 26, brought the largest cargo of the season — about 1,800,000 pounds. The *Eudora*, which arrived in the Inlet on November 19, and the *Frieda Gramph*, which followed in January, 1887, each carried about 1,000,000 pounds. In all, the seven vessels brought over 176,000 packages of tea, together with small shipments of curios and rice, totalling about 4,000 tons weight and about 9,000 tons measurement — a most acceptable addition to the transcontinental freight traffic of a young railway system.

Everett Frazar, senior partner of Frazar & Company, visited Vancouver in September, 1886, on behalf of his own firm and a number of insurance agencies. He declared himself well pleased with the facilities of the Inlet and compared conditions favourably with those at Portland, to which Frazar & Company had also dispatched a number of tea ships. He stated that no further vessels would be sent to the Columbia, as towing costs there were much higher and the river-bars made navigation hazardous. He was convinced that a regular steamer service to the Orient would be a profitable venture, and thought that it should be able to capture a large share of the trans-Pacific silk trade, almost all of which was routed at the time through San Francisco.[5]

A steamship service was exactly what the Canadian Pacific was determined to secure. The chartering of sailing ships was never regarded as anything but a stop-gap; and, pending the outcome of its negotiations with the Dominion and Imperial authorities for a mail subsidy, the Company arranged for a temporary service. Early in 1887 it became known that three old Cunard liners — the *Abyssinia, Parthia* and *Batavia* — had been secured to run between Vancouver and the Orient. The circumstances which brought these particular steamers to the Pacific are not without interest, for they arose from the intense rivalry for the Atlantic record. In the late sixties the Cunard Company had come to the conclusion that the game was not worth the candle; and during the next ten years no steamers comparable to the best ships possessed by rival lines were added to the Cunard fleet. By the end of that period, however, it had become evident that economy could be an expensive policy and that the famous old line must either build a new express fleet or suffer total eclipse. Two fine new steamers did much to restore the prestige of the Cunard flag; but their margin of superiority over rival liners was a narrow one. It was decided, therefore, to place an order for two additional steamers with the yard which had built the fastest of the competing liners — John Elder & Company, of Govan, Scotland. At this time the Elder Company was controlled by Sir William Pearce, who had started his career as a naval architect, but had later become not only a famous ship-builder, but a noted owner and manager of ships as well. The construction of its new liners taxed the resources of the Cunard Company to the utmost; and it was arranged that three of the older units of the fleet should be handed over to the shipyard as part payment for the new ships — an arrangement made possible by the diverse interests of Sir William Pearce. Thus it came about that the *Abyssinia, Parthia,* and *Batavia* passed into the hands of Pearce and his associates before the completion of the new *Umbria* and *Etruria*, in 1885.

All three steamers had been built on the Clyde in 1870 — the *Batavia* and *Parthia* by the famous firm of Denny, at Dumbarton, and the Abyssinia by the Thomson yard at Clydebank. Steel ships were then still in the experimental stage, so their stout old hulls were of iron. Their small size will amaze the ocean traveller of today. The *Abyssinia*, largest of the three, was only 363.5 feet long and 42.2 feet wide, with a gross tonnage of 3,651. As fitted for Cunard service she could carry 200 first-class and 868 steerage passengers. The *Parthia* resembled the *Abyssinia* in general design, but she was not a sister ship, as is often stated. Her length was 360.5 feet, her width 40.4 feet, and her gross tonnage 3,431. The *Batavia* was very different, not only in size but also in appearance, for she had a clipper bow instead of a straight stem. She was not of Cunard design, having been built as a speculation by the shipyard and sold to the Company. Her length was 327.4 feet, her width 39.3 feet, and her gross tonnage only 2,553 — less than half that of several of the *Princess* steamers which later sailed between Victoria and Vancouver.

The three steamers were overhauled at the Elder yard, where the *Parthia* received new triple-expansion engines, which increased her speed. They were then assigned to the Guion Line, which Sir William Pearce controlled; but he was well aware that they were no longer suitable for the Atlantic trade. From his point of view, the demand for a steamer service from Vancouver to the Orient was thus most opportune. The old Cunarders were capable of meeting immediate needs and an agreement was soon reached between Pearce and the Canadian Pacific. Pearce retained control of the steamers, but undertook to operate them upon a route and schedule which met the needs of the Railway; while the appointment of Adamson, Bell & Company to act both as managers of the ships and as agents for the Canadian Pacific in the Orient ensured the necessary unity of action. The new service was known as the "Canadian Pacific Steamship Line" but it had no corporate connection with the Railway.

It was announced at first that the *Parthia* would inaugurate the new service; but in the end it was the *Abyssinia* which sailed from Hong Kong on May 17, 1887, and from Yokohama on May 31, as the pioneer steamship bound for British Columbia. By the latter date preparations for her arrival on the other side of the Pacific had been completed. Port Moody had lost its fight to prevent the transfer of the railway terminus to a point farther down Burrard Inlet, and the first transcontinental train reached Vancouver on May 23.

In February the Canadian Pacific had called for tenders for the construction of a 500-foot addition to its Vancouver wharf. Work commenced in March and the new wharf, complete with freight-shed and baggage-room, was ready for use two months later. On May 28 the *News-Advertiser* noted that the previous day the steamship *Willamette* had had "the distinguished honor of discharging the first full cargo at the C.P.R. wharf."

Abysinnia : arriving Vancouver, June 14, 1887.

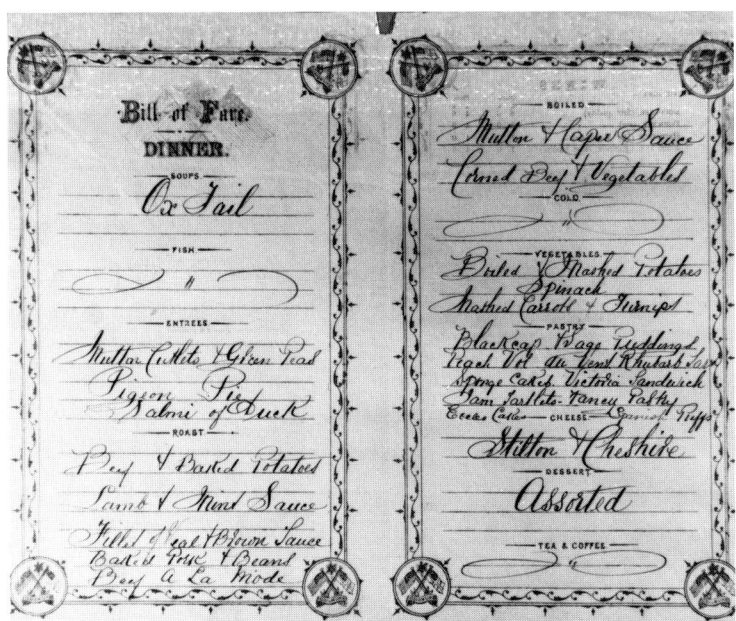

Abysinnia : under operation by Guion Line; inside pages of menu of 1882.

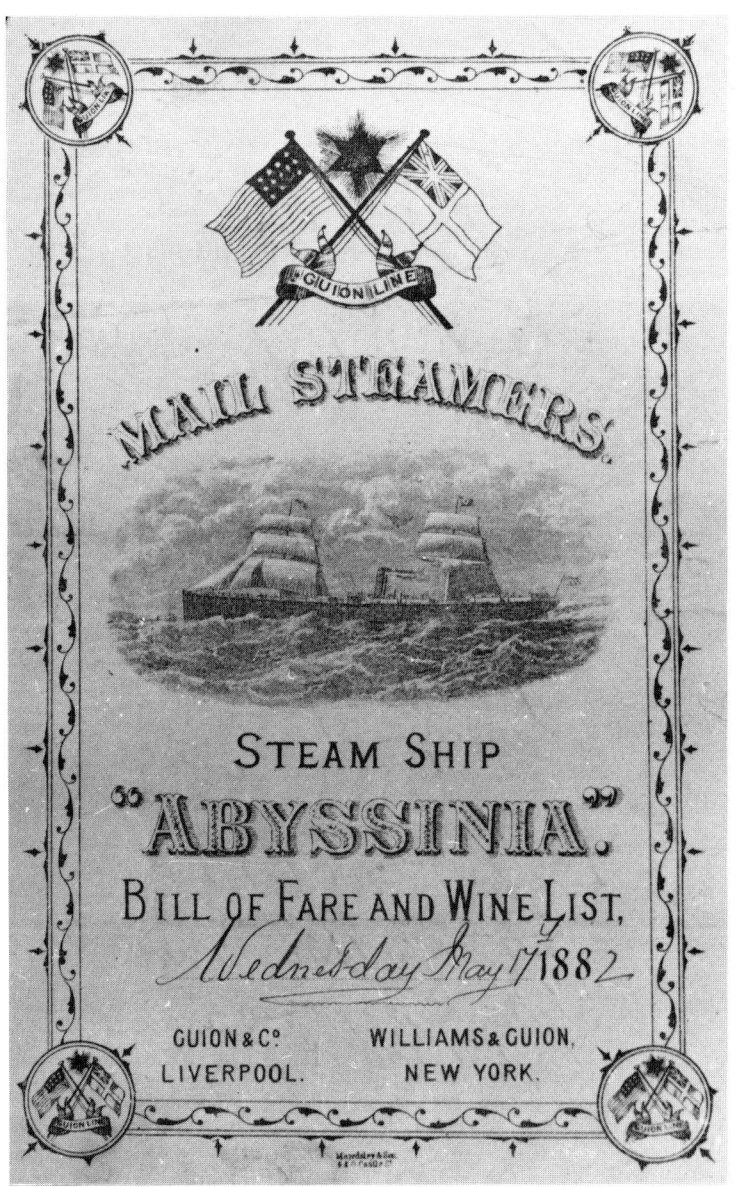

Abyssinia : front cover of menu of 1882.

Abyssinia at C.P.R. dock, Vancouver, July 1, 1887.

Abyssinia : unloading tea, Vancouver.

The *Abyssinia* arrived in the straits on the afternoon of June 13; and the telegram announcing that she had been sighted caused much excitement in Vancouver. "Preparations were now made to give the pioneer vessel a hearty welcome," the *News-Advertiser* reported the next day. "The City Council met and immediately adjourned, the Mayor and most of the aldermen making their way down to the wharf. Presently the strains of music were heard, and the City Band went marching down the street, playing lively airs, towards the wharf. By this time hundreds of people were congregated on the wharf, along Water street and on every point affording a good view of the Inlet." As darkness fell many of the buildings were illuminated; but all these preparations were made in vain. Hour after hour passed and there was no sign of the *Abyssinia*; and by 11:30 there was no one left on the wharf but the nightwatchman." Five minutes after midnight the lights of the small steamer *Eliza*, which had gone out with Company officials and others to meet the liner, were seen rounding Brockton Point; and when she docked it was learned that the *Abyssinia* had anchored in English Bay at 9:25 p.m.[6] Some time in the early morning of June 14 she entered the harbour and tied up at the new Canadian Pacific wharf.[7]

Abyssinia: Yokohama, July, 1889 - Inset: Captain Marshall.

The *Abyssinia* was commanded by Captain Alexander Marshall, who reported an uneventful passage of thirteen days fourteen hours from Yokohama. She brought twenty-two first-class passengers — a capacity list, as her cabin accommodation had been much reduced when she was overhauled — and eighty Chinese steerage. The first trans-Pacific mail consisted of three bags of letters and eleven packages of newspapers. Her cargo totalled 2,830 tons measurement and consisted mostly of tea, the bulk of which was consigned to Chicago and New York. Smaller shipments were consigned to Montreal and a number of other Eastern Canadian and American cities. The *Abyssinia* also carried a pioneer silk shipment made up of sixty-three packages for New York and two for Montreal. She carried curios for Eastern centres, and 1,217 packages of general merchandise for Vancouver and Victoria.[8]

A few days after her arrival, Captain Marshall entertained the Mayor and City Council at dinner on board the *Abyssinia*. Those present included Captain Henry Webber, Vancouver representative of Adamson, Bell & Company; J.A. Fullerton, Canadian Pacific marine superintendent; and D.E. Brown, freight agent for the Railway. At least one of the speeches delivered was to some extent prophetic, for, when called upon to say a few words, Dr. Lefevre responded with the suggestion that the C.P.R. should "work up a new industry in bringing the wheat of the great North West to Vancouver, where mills could be erected to grind it, and from thence distribute to our Eastern Hemisphere, for which suggestion Mr. Brown expressed his thankfulness, and made a note of the same."[9]

As in the case of the *W.B. Flint*, the tea brought by the *Abyssinia* was hurried across the continent in order to demonstrate the efficiency of the new Canadian route from the Orient. Part of her cargo arrived in Montreal on June 27, only twenty-seven days from Yokohama; and shipments reached New York two days later. Meanwhile a more sensational record had been established by a small trial parcel of tea which reached New York on June 21, caught the liner *City of Rome*, and was delivered in London on June 29, having travelled from Japan in only twenty-nine days.[10]

The *Abyssinia* cleared for the Orient on June 20; and a fortnight later, on July 4, the *Parthia*, second of the trans-Pacific steamers to arrive, tied up at Vancouver. She was commanded by Captain Charles Brough and carried 37 first-class and 110 steerage passengers. Her cargo totalled 2,975 tons measurement and consisted of a very large shipment of tea, over 5,000 sacks of rice, 36 bales of silk, and a quantity of miscellaneous goods.[11] These figures and those relating to the *Abyssinia* have been quoted because they are representative of the cargoes which were brought to Vancouver during the next few years, and thus indicate the general character of the trade which developed. The steamers usually arrived in Vancouver well laden, and capacity cargoes were not infrequent. On the other hand, the volume of trade outward was much smaller, though fairly regular shipments of a few staple articles soon appeared. The most important of these was flour, most of which was brought from Portland in coastal steamers and trans-shipped at Vancouver. The *Abyssinia* carried a small quantity on her first westbound voyage; but the first large shipment was sent in the *Parthia*. Cotton goods consigned to China from the Eastern United States also became an important item; and 1,500 bales were shipped by the third ship to enter the new service, the *Port Augusta*. The latter was a new 2,833-ton steamer owned by Milburn & Company, of Newcastle, and had been chartered to make one round trip to Vancouver in place of the *Batavia*, which was not yet available. Another Milburn ship, the *Port Victor*, of 2,793 tons, made a similar voyage later in the year.

When the *Parthia* reached Vancouver for the second time, on August 20, her passengers included Sir Francis and Lady Plunkett. Sir Francis was then British Minister to Japan and he seems to have been the first distinguished personage to travel by the new Canadian Pacific route. On her return passage the *Parthia* carried the first royal patrons of the line — the brother of the King of Siam and his four small sons, who were homeward bound after attending Queen Victoria's Jubilee in London. The new service was attracting much attention, and this was reflected in a keen local interest in the steamers and their movements. We are told that the second arrival of the *Parthia* "was witnessed by an immense crowd of people, who required all the efforts of the C.P.R. employees to keep them from crowding in the way of the men at the wharf"; and that gates had to be erected to prevent a repetition of this trouble in future.[12] Local pride in the line led to exaggerated conceptions of the size and grandeur of the ships themselves; and Captan Urquhart, who piloted them in and out, became a popular hero. Thus we read that, when the *Parthia* sailed in November, "the way in which he handled the enormous mass was a source of admiration to the crowds of spectators who had assembled to see the vessel sail."[13] One grasps the scale of the picture better when one notes that owing to the fact that the *Parthia* "brought ten sacks of mail matter for different points," Postmaster Miller and his assistants were kept busy sorting all night![14]

Tacoma ex *Batavia*, 1898.

George B. Dodwell.

The *Batavia* did not enter service until late in the year; and it was on December 27 that she reached Vancouver, after a phenomenally rough passage from Yokohama lasting almost seventeen days. She was the ninth and last arrival in 1887. According to George B. Dodwell, who was a partner in Adamson, Bell & Company at the time, the service was operated during this first season at a loss;[15] but the Canadian Pacific was satisfied with its progress and prospects. The temporary service, in the words of the report to shareholders, had "fully justified the expectations of your Directors as to the value and importance of the trade to be developed in that direction."[16]

Meanwhile the negotiations for a subsidy, though on the point of success, still hung fire. Lord Salisbury was again Prime Minister and in the autumn the Imperial Government notified the Canadian Pacific that it was prepared to grant an annual subsidy of £60,000 for a monthly service from Vancouver to Japan and China. Details were settled by December, but one difficulty still prevented the signing of a contract. The existing steamer line from Great Britain to Canada was much too slow to form a satisfactory part of the new all-British route to the Orient; and the British Government was unwilling to subsidize a fast Pacific service until an improved Atlantic service to supplement it became assured. The problem did not concern the Canadian Pacific directly, for the Company had no intention of entering the Atlantic trade at the time; but its contract was held up nevertheless.

There were nineteen Canadian Pacific sailings from Vancouver to the Orient in 1888, thirteen of which were taken by the regular liners *Abyssinia*, *Parthia*, and *Batavia*. One night in the autumn the *Batavia* rescued two shipwrecked Japanese in a violent storm in the China Sea, but for the most part their voyages were uneventful. Under the command of Captain George A. Lee, who had succeeded Captain Marshall, the *Abyssinia* crossed the Pacific in May at an average speed of 13 1/4 knots, which was a record for the line; but the *Parthia* later proved to be the fastest of the trio and upon occasion arrived as much as two days ahead of time.

Parthia: unloading tea, Vancouver, 1887.

Parthia : bell, (Museum of History and Industry, Seattle.)

Parthia: C.P.R. dock, Vancouver.

The six extra sailings were taken by chartered steamers, made necessary by the growth of the trans-Pacific trade. The first to arrive was the *Zambesi*, an old P. & O. liner of 2,421 tons. She was followed by the *Port Adelaide* and the *Albany*, the latter of which made two voyages. The remaining two sailings were made by more notable craft — the *Aberdeen* and the *Duke of Westminster*. The former was a ship of some historical interest, as she was the first large steamship fitted with triple-expansion engines. They proved a great success, which led to general adoption of the principle. The *Aberdeen* was of 3,616 tons gross, which made her the largest steamer which had yet entered Burrard Inlet; and she bettered this record by bringing the largest cargo yet landed — 3,425 tons measurement. It consisted of 2,417 tons of tea, 1,007 tons of general merchandise, and 237 packages of silk. When she sailed outward the *Aberdeen* carried 25,000 sacks of flour, 2,125 bales of cotton goods, and a quantity of paper and machinery, totalling in all about 1,200 tons.[17] It will be noticed that the character of the trade had altered little since the pioneer voyages of the *Abyssinia* and *Parthia*.

The *Duke of Westminster* broke the port records once again, for she was of 3,726 tons gross and her cargo totalled 3,844 tons measurement. She, too, has a place in shipping history, for she ran ashore near the Isle of Wight, pounded on the rocks for a week, and confounded the critics of steel ships by neither cracking a plate nor starting a rivet.

But the great event of 1888 was not the mere coming and going of ships, but the invasion of the San Francisco trade by the Canadian Pacific. At this time neither Portland, Tacoma, nor Seattle had any regular connection with the Orient. American trans-Pacific trade was almost exclusively in the hands of two lines running out of San

Francisco — the old-established Pacific Mail Company, which had started the first trans-Pacific steamer service in 1867, and the Oriental & Occidental Line, which operated a number of chartered White Star steamers. Working agreements linked the O. & O. with the Pacific Mail, and control of the latter was divided between the Union Pacific and Southern Pacific Railways.[18] Nothing daunted by this imposing combine, the Canadian Pacific determined to try and secure a share of the San Francisco freight trade, and also of the Chinese passenger trade, which was increasing rapidly. When the *Parthia* reached Vancouver on April 9, she carried freight and Chinese for San Francisco, and proceeded thither on the 12th. A month later the *Abyssinia* arrived with no less than 625 passengers, 590 of them Chinese, most of which she took to San Francisco. All during the summer the steamers averaged more than 600 passengers a voyage, the record list of 708 being brought by the *Batavia* in June. In all, twelve steamers sailed south between April and October; but in the latter month the service ceased as abruptly as it had commenced. Its usefulness had ended, for an exclusion order had ruined the Chinese steerage trade, and certain traffic concessions had been secured from the American railroads.

Chinese steerage passengers on deck of a C.P.R. ship.

The matter did not end there, for exaggerated reports of the traffic handled by the Canadian Pacific sprang up on every hand. In August, 1888, Senator Cullom, of Illinois, persuaded the United States Senate to appoint a committee to investigate the whole question of competition from Canadian transportation lines.[19] A long inquiry followed, in the course of which officials of most of the companies concerned gave evidence, including W.C. Van Horne, who appeared on behalf of the Canadian Pacific. The voluminous report of the committee was printed in 1890, and many interesting facts regarding the trans-Pacific trade can be found in its pages.[20] Attention was directed to the volume of United States imports from Japan and China which had been routed via Canadian Pacific steamers and rail lines. This had been tabulated by consular representatives, who reported that in 1888 560,591 pounds of raw silk, 216,385 pounds of rice, and no less than 14,687,627 pounds of tea had been shipped in this way.[21] Van Horne's comment upon these figures is interesting. "Our business from China and Japan," he told the committee, "has been taken almost wholly from the Suez Canal. There is more business done between San Francisco and Tacoma and China and Japan than before we opened. But the trade between China and Japan and Canada and the United States, via the Suez Canal, has fallen off 75 per cent since we opened. The business we do is not done at the expense of the American lines." On the contrary, competition had probably helped them by stirring them to greater activity. "I think the [trans-Pacific] traffic has doubled over any period before we opened."[22]

Westbound, the chief American exports carried by the Canadian steamers were flour and cotton goods. Little was said about the former, but careful attention was paid to the cotton trade. During the year ended June 30, 1888, it appeared that 4,660,168 pounds of cotton goods had been carried, and in the succeeding twelve months the total had jumped to 11,756,504 pounds.[23] In addition, heavy shipments of English cotton goods had been landed at Montreal and shipped thence to China. In defence of the Canadian Pacific, even American witnesses admitted that the cotton trade was a new development, and that the through rates and rapid transit the line could offer gave the Canadian route important advantages.

It appeared, in the final analysis, that it was the American railways, rather than the steamer lines, which lost traffic to the Canadian

Pacific. It was true that the steamers no longer had a monopoly, but, in spite of competition, the traffic they handled had increased. On the other hand, the Union Pacific and Southern Pacific had been compelled to assign a definite share of the transcontinental freight originating in the Orient to the Canadian Pacific. It was estimated that of the total traffic that Tacoma and the Northern Pacific Railway handled about 12 per cent, Vancouver and the Canadian Pacific about 27 per cent, and San Francisco and the southern lines about 60 per cent.[24]

Great interest was taken in Vancouver in the arrival and departure of the trans-Pacific steamers; and fairly complete traffic statistics can be compiled from the newspapers. The cargoes carried on fifteen of nineteen inward voyages in 1888 totalled 32,401 tons measurement; and assuming that the average size of the unrecorded cargoes was the same as those on record,[25] the total for the year was approximately 41,000 tons. Cargo carried outward on thirteen voyages totalled 17,721 tons, or about 24,500 tons in the twelve months. Applying this method to other figures available, it is possible to arrive at the following totals:

INWARD VOYAGES — TONS MEASUREMENT

1888 - 15 recorded cargoes, 32,401 tons; 19 voyages (about), 41,000 tons
1889 - 17 recorded cargoes, 32,350 tons; 18 voyages (about), 34,250 tons
1890 - 17 recorded cargoes, 34,169 tons; 18 voyages (about), 36,000 tons

OUTWARD VOYAGES — TONS MEASUREMENT

1888 - 13 recorded cargoes, 17,721 tons; 18 voyages (about), 24,500 tons
1889 - 12 recorded cargoes, 16,674 tons; 18 voyages (about), 25,000 tons
1890 - 10 recorded cargoes, 22,131 tons; 17 voyages (about), 37,600 tons

It will be noted that the outward cargoes are less carefully recorded, and less reliance can therefore be placed upon the annual estimates given. The estimate of 37,600 tons for 1890 is probably high; but a number of heavy shipments were made that year, and on March 18 the *Abyssinia* sailed with a cargo of some 2,100 tons weight and 4,000 tons measurement, which broke the port record by a considerable margin. From the figures available it is evident that over the three-year period 1888-1890 the average inward cargo consisted of about 2,020 tons measurement, while outward cargoes averaged about 1,615 tons.

Passenger lists were usually noted for the inward voyages and the following totals appear to be substantially correct:

	First Class	Second Class	Steerage	Total
1887	220	13	361	594
1888*	252	51	6,087	6,390
1889	293	34	1,156	1,483
1890	279	39	1.947	2.265

* Includes only seventeen of eighteen sailings, but figures lacking would be small.

+ Mostly Chinese booked to San Francisco.

Outbound passenger lists were often not reported, and totals corresponding to those above cannot be given with any confidence. Generally speaking, the volume of travel to the Orient seems to have been only slightly lower than that eastbound, except in the exceptional year 1888, when thousands of Chinese were carried to San Francisco.

The Canadian Pacific was satisfied with the freight traffic, but it hoped for greater things from the passenger trade. "The freight traffic to and from China and Japan continues to increase," the Directors reported early in 1889, "but the steamships forming the present temporary line on the Pacific have accommodation for very few passengers, and the passenger business in that direction, which should afford to the railway far greater profit than the freight, is consequently limited."[26] The truth was that after the first burst of interest in the new route had subsided, the old Cunarders found it difficult to compete with more modern steamers on other routes. Though their accommodation was enlarged and improved from time to time, and they acquired a reputation for cleanliness and courteous service, their design remained cramped and antiquated. Quite as serious, it proved almost impossible to keep them up to time; and again and again it was necessary to cancel schedules and revise sailings. There is significance as well as humour in an incident recorded by a traveller who sailed in 1888 from Vancouver: "Nobody ever knows to an hour or so, just when a China steamer means to depart, and we had heard the farewell whistle so frequently before, that it did not in the least occur to us, as we lingered in town buying blue veils and pickled olives for the voyage, that she could be blowing it five times for us. It is an original experience to be hunted up by an angry emissary in a cab, [and] to be driven down post haste through the rain to the docks..."[27]

What was required to attract and develop the passenger trade was a fast, reliable service performed by comfortable modern steamers; and the long-delayed signing of a mail contract with the Imperial Government in July, 1889, at last made it possible for the Canadian Pacific to build the necessary liners. The contract called for a monthly service from Vancouver to Yokohama, Shanghai and Hong Kong, to be performed by steamers built to specifications approved by the Admiralty and capable of a sustained sea speed of at least 16 knots. In return the Company was to receive an annual subsidy of £ 60,000, of which £ 15,000 was provided by the Canadian Government. The Canadian Pacific went ahead with its plans at once, and early in October three steamers were ordered from the Naval Construction and Armaments Company of Barrow, England. It is ironical to note that preliminary arrangements for a fast Atlantic line to Canada, the completion of which had induced the British Government to sign the Canadian Pacific contract, collapsed only a few days later.

There were eighteen sailings from Vancouver in 1889, of which fourteen were taken by the regular liners. In addition, the steamers *Port Augusta* and *Port Fairy* each made two voyages. Early in January word arrived that Sir William Pearce, virtual owner of the service, had died on December 18; and a blue streak was painted forthwith on the sides of the *Parthia*, which was in port at the time, as a sign of mourning.[28] Rumour was busy during the year with reports of new trans-Pacific services. In February one of the managers of the Nippon Yusen Kaisha visited Vancouver and inferred that the Company might enter the trade. In June it was announced that the P. & O. Line had completed arrangements for a service to San Diego which would connect with the Santa Fe Railway. The diversion of trade from the Suez Canal to the Canadian Pacific had been accomplished partly at the expense of the P. & O., and such a move would not have been surprising. More was heard of the proposal at various times, but in the end it came to nothing. Late in 1889 the Canadian Pacific was faced with an unexpected crisis, due to the fact that its new steamers were to be built by the Naval Construction Company. The Elder yard, which had by then developed into the Fairfield Shipbuilding & Engineering Company, had expected to receive the contract, and threatened to withdraw the *Abyssinia, Parthia* and *Batavia* at the end of November, when the current running agreement with the railway expired; but tempers cooled rapidly and the service continued without interruption.[29]

The Pacific Mail remained the chief competitor of the Canadian Pacific, and early in 1890 another clash between the two was impending. Though none of its trans-Pacific steamers had called at San Francisco since 1888, the Canadian Pacific had placed the smaller *Danube* in the coastal trade in August of that year.[30] She was used chiefly to bring flour from Portland, but upon occasion ventured farther south. The Pacific Mail prepared for eventualities by building the new liner *China*, which entered service in November, 1889. She was built by the Fairfield Company, at a cost of $826,000, and was the finest trans-Pacific steamer of her day. Early in 1890 it became known that the Pacific Mail was negotiating with the Northern Pacific Railway regarding a service from Tacoma to the Orient; and with this scheme in the air it was not surprising that when its traffic agreement with the Canadian Pacific expired, a rate war followed. Upon this occasion it was the Pacific Mail which took the initiative and instructed its steamers to call at Victoria. The first to arrive was the new *China*, which anchored off the outer wharf on August 2, picked up six passengers, and proceeded to the Orient. A few days later the inbound *City of Peking* called and landed 108 passengers; but by the time she reached San Francisco the rival lines had patched up their differences. A belated call by the *City of Rio de Janeiro* in September brought the episode to a close, for little more was heard of the Tacoma project.

Victoria ex *Parthia*: Vancouver, 1901.

Extra steamers were again required in 1890 to handle the growing trade between the Orient and Vancouver. The *Sussex* made one trip and the *Straits of Belle Isle* two. The latter struck the wharf when docking at Vancouver in August, but no great damage was done. This was one of only three minor mishaps suffered by ships of the line in its pioneer days. In November the *Abyssinia* touched bottom in the Narrows, but a diver found her to be unharmed, except for a slightly bent propeller. An amusing controversy followed as to whether or not she had struck a water-main, which had been crushed mysteriously the day she sailed.

Abyssinia : at Vancouver with Duke and Duchess of Connaught, May, 1890.

The third mishap occurred to the *Batavia*. When making a special trip to Portland she grounded in the Willamette River, but was refloated undamaged. In May, 1890, the *Abyssinia* arrived from the Orient with the Duke and Duchess of Connaught on board, and received a royal welcome both at Victoria, where she made a special call, and Vancouver. In November of the same year the *Parthia* brought the first shipment of raw sugar for the new refinery at Vancouver, which was due to commence operations a month later.

Meanwhile the construction of the new trans-Pacific steamers was proceeding in England; and on August 30, 1890, the first of the trio slid down the ways and was named *Empress of India*. By the end of the year she and her sister ships, the *Empress of Japan* and *Empress of China*, were nearing completion; and early in 1891 the old chartered liners began to drop out of the service. On January 28 the pioneer of the line, the *Abyssinia*, sailed from Vancouver for the seventeenth and last time. Ten days later, on February 8, her successor, the *Empress of India*, sailed from Liverpool on her maiden voyage, carrying a large party of round-the-world excursionists. Late in March the *Batavia* made her last Canadian Pacific sailing, which completed her fifteenth round trip in the service. With her departure the contract with the Fairfield interests expired; but the *Parthia* was retained under special charter pending the arrival of all three *Empresses*. It is interesting to note that on this final crossing of the original schedule the *Batavia* carried a capacity cargo, and that her passengers included Captain Marshall, who had commanded the *Abyssinia* on her first voyage in 1887, and who had since become manager of the Guion Line, which operated the ships for the Fairfield Company.

The *Empress of India* arrived at Vancouver on April 28, 1891, after a fast maiden voyage which broke the Pacific record. She carried 131 first-class passengers and 355 Chinese—a list which must have gladdened the heart of Van Horne, who was on the wharf when she docked. Her arrival caused great excitement in Vancouver, but some present sensed that the occasion fell short of the arrival of the line's pioneer ship four years before. As the *News-Advertiser* remarked in an editorial, it was "impossible to bring about again an enthusiasm like that which found popular vent on that day in May [sic], in 1887, when a brief telegram to the *News-Advertiser* announced that the *Abyssinia* had passed Victoria and would arrive in Vancouver in a few hours. Then men felt that the period of suspense and difficulty which beset the earlier months of the existence of the city was at an end."[31] The *Abyssinia* had been a symbol, whereas the *Empress* was only a new and finer trans-Pacific liner.

Empress of India: arriving Vancouver, April 28, 1891.

Illuminated Address to William Van Horne from Mayor and Council of Vancouver on the occasion of the arrival of *Empress of India*, April 28, 1891.

The *Empress of Japan* reached Vancouver in June and the *Empress of China* followed in September. Chartered steamers were no longer required and on August 20 the *Parthia* sailed on her twentieth and last voyage for the Railway. She had been the most satisfactory of the three pioneers and had won a place in Vancouver's affections; and as she left the dock for the last time "a number of rockets were shot off as a last farewell."[32]

The subsequent history of the three pioneer liners is worthy of record. The *Abyssinia* loaded a cargo of tea at Hong Kong and carried it to London, where she arrived in September. She was then placed in the trans-Atlantic trade by the Guion Line. On December 13, 1891 — a date of which the superstitious will take note — she sailed from New York for Liverpool, carrying fifty-six passengers and a crew of eighty. All went well until noon on the 18th, when the vessel took fire; and a few hours later flames broke through the deck and it became clear the ship was doomed. It appears to have been a model shipwreck. The life-boats were carefully provisioned and all aboard were given a substantial meal; and at the critical moment when it became necessary to abandon ship the North German Lloyd express liner *Spree* appeared and picked up the passengers and crew. All were landed safely at Southampton on December 22, having reached England several days before the slower *Abyssinia* was due.

Much longer careers lay ahead of the *Batavia* and *Parthia*. The former was first chartered by the Upton Line, which a Mr. Frank Upton established between Portland, Victoria, and the Orient in 1891. The *Batavia* made four round trips in this service, her last sailing from Victoria being on April 30, 1892. By that time the Upton Line was on the point of collapse, and it ceased operations in the course of the summer. The *Batavia* was only idle for a brief period, however, as a new trans-Pacific service with more substantial backing was organized in May. This was the Northern Pacific Steamship Company, which was managed by George B. Dodwell and his associates, who had previously operated the temporary service for the Canadian Pacific. Despite its name, it was neither owned nor controlled by the Northern Pacific Railway, though it connected with the latter at Tacoma and had traffic agreements with it. The *Batavia* was taken over immediately by the new line and called at Victoria on her first inward voyage on July 6. Dodwell also arranged to place the *Parthia* on the run. Like the *Abyssinia*, she had been sent to Great Britain; but instead of being placed in the Atlantic trade she was turned over to the Fairfield yard to be extensively rebuilt and modernized. Finally, when it was arranged that she was to enter the Northern Pacific service, she was renamed *Victoria*, with the result that she received an official welcome when she called at the city of that name for the first time on September 19. Meanwhile the *Batavia* had been taken in hand and refitted at Hong Kong; and in December, 1892, she made her first voyage under the new name of *Tacoma*.

The *Victoria* and *Tacoma* continued in regular service to the Orient for the next six years. Then in October, 1898, they were transferred from British to United States registry; and in 1899 were requisitioned as transports during the Spanish-American War. In September the *Victoria* sailed from Tacoma with horses, bound for Manila by way of Dutch Harbor, Alaska, and Kobe. Late in November she sailed with a second load from Seattle; but over 200 of the 410 horses on board were lost in a storm and she was forced back to port. She made her third and last trip as a transport from San Francisco in December, and was turned back to her owners in March, 1900. A few months later the Nome gold excitement took her off her regular run once again; and on June 7 she sailed from Seattle for Cape Nome with no less than 1,200 passengers. From Nome she proceeded to Yokohama and resumed her place in the trans-Pacific service.[33]

In 1901 the Northern Pacific Railway itself organized a new Northern Pacific Steamship Company, which later in the year purchased the *Victoria*, *Tacoma* and other vessels. In 1902 ownership of the line was transferred to the Northwestern Improvement Company, another Northern Pacific subsidiary. By this time it was clear that the steamers were too small to compete successfully in the trans-Pacific trade; and in February, 1904, they were sold to the Northwestern Commercial Company, of Seattle, of which John Rosene was President. The *Victoria* and *Tacoma* were placed on the Alaska run in June; and in August the *Victoria* sailed on a special excursion to Alaska and Siberia, where Rosene had mining interests.

War had broken out between Russia and Japan just before Rosene purchased the steamers; and even at the time it was said that it was his intention to use them as blockade runners between Alaskan and Russian ports.[34] Whether this was true or not is difficult to say; but the fact remains that the *Tacoma* was used eventually for this purpose. On January 3, 1905, she sailed from Seattle with a cargo of corned beef, under the command of Captain Connaughton. Ostensibly her destination was Shanghai; but January 14 found her calling at Dutch Harbor, and on February 3 she was caught in the ice in the Sea of Okhotsk. She was soon observed by the Japanese; and on March 14, when she managed to work clear of the ice, was boarded by the cruiser *Takachiho*, which escorted her first to Hakodate for coal and then to Yokohama, where she was formally taken over as a prize and placed under the Japanese flag on March 29.[35] It is said that she was used for a time as a training-ship; but she spent most of her later years in the Japanese and Chinese coasting trade under the name of *Shikotan Maru*. In October, 1924, she ran ashore while carrying coal from Tsingtau to Shanghai; and though she was subsequently refloated, she was broken up soon after.[36] So ended her long and eventful career of some fifty-five years.

Meanwhile the *Victoria* continued in the Alaska trade. In 1908 the Northwestern Steamship Company was merged with the Alaska Steamship Company, under the latter name, and the *Victoria* flew its house flag for nearly forty years. For many of them her regular run was to Nome, and she was usually the first ship to reach that port in spring and the last to leave it in the autumn. In 1923-24 she was fitted for oil fuel and her accommodation was extensively rebuilt; her stout old iron hull had been reinforced to enable her to cope with the ice she occasionally encountered in the north.

During a maritime strike in the winter of 1936-37 she was tied up for several months at a pier in Vancouver, but few people recalled that she was the old *Parthia*. She next spent some time in reserve, but the Second World War brought her out of retirement and from 1941 to 1947 she returned to the Alaska run under the control of the U.S. War Shipping Administration. By that time she had become a freighter. It was clear that her long career was coming to an end, but the Alaska Line retained her in reserve until 1954, when she was sold to the Dulien Steel Products Company of Seattle for scrapping. Her hull was converted into a barge and sold to the Straits Towing Company of Vancouver, who named it *Straits No. 27*. Perhaps this was an indignity that the *Parthia* resented; in any event, her hull proved to be too unwieldy for towing, and in 1956 it was sold to Japanese shipbreakers. The remains of the *Parthia*, loaded with scrap metal, made the last of many trans-Pacific voyages at the end of a tow rope, under the name *Straits Maru*.

She was then 86 years old. Few steamers have matched her astonishing record of long and useful service.

W.B. Flint being burnt for her metal, Seattle, March 18, 1937.

Empress of Japan (1), painted window from Dining Saloon.
Collection: Mr. John A. Claridge.

Empress of Japan (1), painted window from Dining Saloon.
Collection: Mr. John A. Claridge

Empress of India: Illuminated Address to Captain Marshall, 1891.
Collection: Vancouver City Archives.

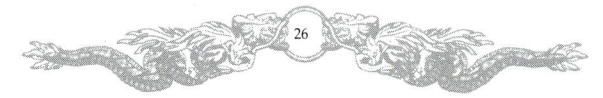

Tacoma ex *Batavia* : oil. Collection: Dr. Wallace B. Chung.

Early C.P.R. wharves, Coal Harbour: watercolour, A. Lee Rogers. Collection: Vancouver Maritime Museum.

C.P.R. station and dock: oil, J.C., 1907.
Collection: Vancouver Maritime Museum.

Empress of India : mixed media on milk glass, J. Bell.
Collection: Vancouver Maritime Museum.

Empress of India: oil, A. Kwan. Private collection.

Port of Nagasaki, 1890's; hand-tinted photograph. Collection: Dr. Wallace B. Chung.

Port of Kobe, 1890's; hand-tinted photograph. Collection: Dr. Wallace B. Chung.

Empress of Japan (1); foremast bell. Collection: Vancouver Maritime Museum.

II.

EMPRESS TO THE ORIENT 1892 - 1912

Just a century ago the hulls of three steamships destined to make history on the Pacific Ocean were taking shape amid the bustle and noise of a busy English shipyard. These vessels were the three original *Empress* liners, ordered by the Canadian Pacific Railway to take the place of the old chartered steamers which had opened the service between Vancouver and the Orient in 1887.[1]

Work had begun on the *Empresses* some two years later than the Canadian Pacific had hoped and intended. As early as July, 1887, the Company had submitted a tender for the carriage of mails from the Atlantic seaboard to Japan and China, the terms of which differed little from those later accepted by the Imperial Government. By December the details of the agreement were settled; and while these final discussions were in progress the Company had also made preliminary arrangements for the building of the steamers which would be required to fulfil the contract. Indeed, Mr. (later Sir William) Van Horne announced in Vancouver that the Canadian Pacific had actually ordered "three grand new steamers for the trans-Pacific trade,"[2] and later reports stated that they were to be built at the Fairfield yard on the Clyde.[3] These announcements proved premature, however; for, although it was true that agreement had been reached on the terms of the mail subsidy, no contract was signed for another eighteen months. Political considerations were responsible in part for this delay, but it was due primarily to the inadequacy of the existing steamship service between Great Britain and Canada, which was much too slow to form a satisfactory part of a new fast route to the Orient. At last, in 1889, plans for an improved Atlantic service seemed so far advanced that the British Government deemed it prudent to proceed, and the trans-Pacific mail contract was awarded to the Canadian Pacific Railway on July 15.

This contract called for a four-weekly service and covered the carriage of mails across Canada as well as across the Pacific. The time in transit from Halifax or Quebec to Hong Kong was not to exceed twenty-eight and one-half days in summer or thirty and one-half days in winter, and heavy cash penalties were imposed for late departures or arrivals.[4] The steamers employed were to operate between Vancouver and Hong Kong, calling at Yokohama and Shanghai.

Sir William Van Horne.

They were to be designed as auxiliary cruisers, which meant that they were to be provided with gun platforms and built to specifications approved by the Admiralty. Their speed was to be at least 17 1/2 knots on the measured mile and 16 knots at sea. The terms upon which troops and supplies were to be carried, and the ships themselves requisitioned for war service, were also set forth in the contract. In return for meeting these numerous and exacting requirements the Canadian Pacific was to receive an annual subsidy of £60,000, of which the Canadian Government was to pay £15,000. The agreement was for a period of ten years, dating from the initial departure of the first of the new liners from Hong Kong.

Three fast steamers would be required to maintain the new schedule from Vancouver to the Orient, and no time was lost in arranging for their construction. The chartered ships already in service — the famous old pioneer liners *Abyssinia*, *Parthia* and *Batavia* — happened to be owned by the Fairfield Shipbuilding & Engineering Company. Both for this reason, and because, as we have seen, the contract had been all but awarded to the Fairfield yard in 1887, it was expected that the order would be placed with that firm. Instead, to the general surprise, the contract, which was signed on October 12, 1889, went to the Naval Construction and Armament Company, of Barrow-in-Furness. The Fairfield interests were much disappointed and threatened to withdraw the chartered steamers, as it happened that the current running agreement with the Canadian Pacific was about to expire; but tempers cooled rapidly and the service continued without interruption.

Even at this late date the reason for giving the order to Barrow seems fairly clear. The great works at Fairfield, which had grown out of the famous shipyard of John Elder & Company, had owed much in recent years to two men — Sir William Pearce, the chief proprietor, and A.D. Bryce Douglas, the engineering superintendent. But Sir William had died in December, 1888, and some months before his death Bryce Douglas had been persuaded to accept the position of managing director of the yard at Barrow. Between 1879 and 1884 Pearce had built and Douglas had engined the Guion liners *Arizona*, *Alaska* and *Oregon*, and the Cunarders *Etruria* and *Umbria* — the five fastest and most successful Atlantic express steamers of their day. It was an astonishing record, and there was no reason to suppose that Douglas had lost anything of his skill or inventive genius. In a word, everything suggests that the Canadian Pacific order simply migrated with him from the Clyde to Barrow-in-Furness.

It is interesting to speculate upon the origin of the design of the original *Empresses*. We know that it differed radically from that in preparation in 1887, when considerably smaller vessels with a single screw were contemplated.[5] The decision to build larger and more elaborate steamers was probably due to Van Horne, who in the interval had succeeded Sir George Stephen as President of the Canadian Pacific and who took a very great interest personally in the service to the Orient. When the vessels were being planned, Van Horne was represented in England by T. G. Shaughnessy (later Lord Shaughnessy), who understood fully the business requirements of the case, and by Henry Beatty, who could pass upon the design from the point of view of the practical steamship operator. Mr. Beatty, father of Sir Edward, had owned the line of Great Lakes steamers which the Canadian Pacific had purchased.

Turning next to technical matters, it is said that Professor J.H. Biles, the most celebrated naval architect of the day, helped to determine the underwater lines of the hulls of the *Empresses*. So far as appearance is concerned, we need look no further afield than the Inman liner *City of Rome*, the finest ship and greatest failure produced by the Barrow yard before Bryce Douglas assumed its management. She is known to history as one of the most beautiful steamers ever to sail the Atlantic, in spite of the fact that she failed to make her contract speed and was returned to her builders. She had the long clipper bow, the graceful overhanging counter stern, and the yacht-like lines which characterized the *Empresses*, and although she had three funnels and four masts, whereas they had but two funnels and three masts, even in a photograph the resemblance in general design is striking. So far as machinery was concerned, the *Empresses* were, of course, designed by Bryce Douglas. Construction of the machinery was superintended, on behalf of the Canadian Pacific, by James Fowler, who had been in the service of the Allan Line and who was said to have crossed the Atlantic 250 times without the slightest mishap to the machinery in his charge.

Full particulars of the *Empresses* are given in an appendix, and only a few of their principal dimensions need to be repeated here. Their length between perpendiculars was 455.6 feet, but the clipper bow increased their length over all to 485 feet. Their width was 51.2 feet, and their gross tonnage 5,940. By contemporary standards they were large ships, for the largest vessel in regular service on the Atlantic in 1889 registered no more than 10,600 tons.

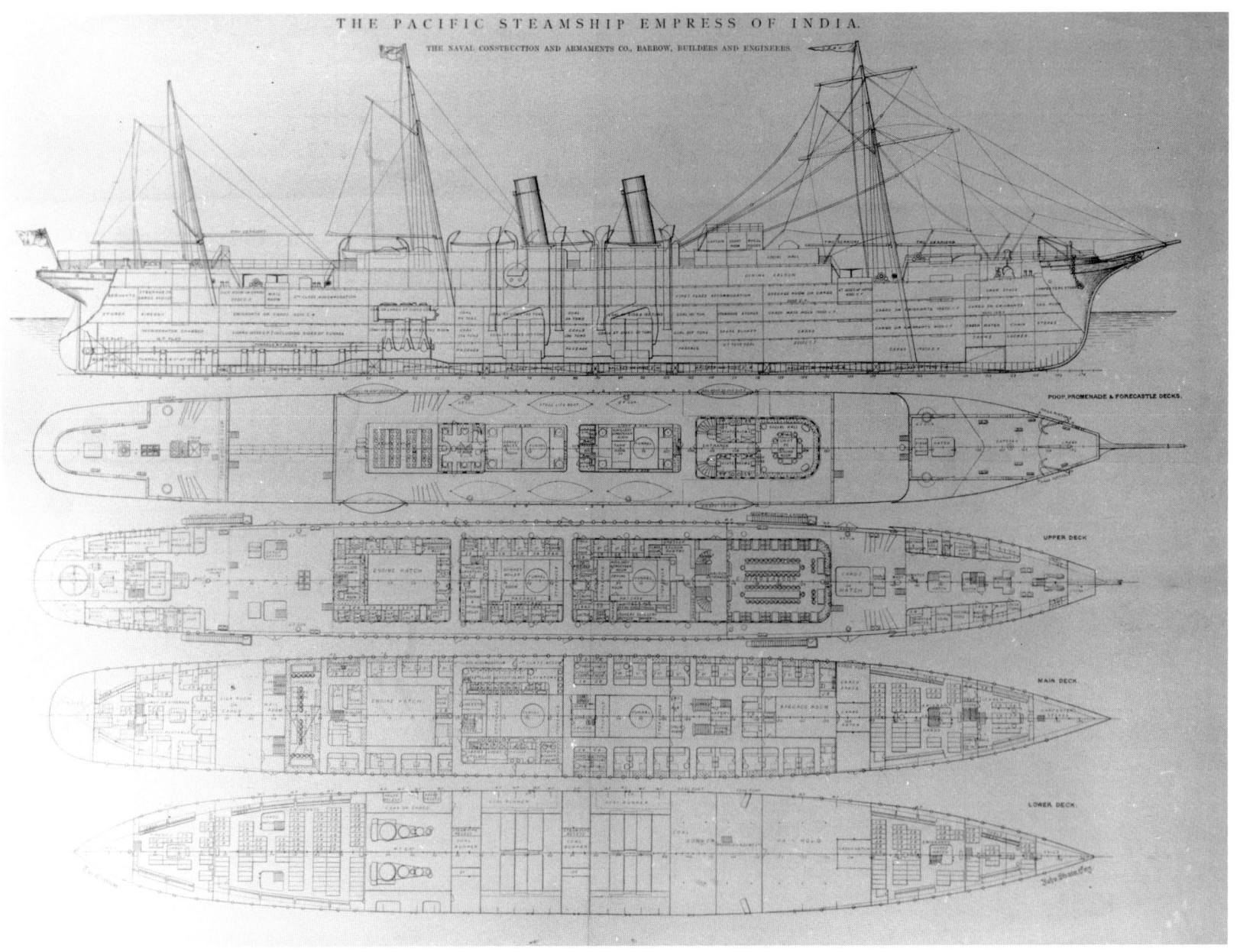

Empress of India: inboard profile and layout of decks.
Collection: Vancouver Maritime Museum.

It will be recalled that the mail contract with the British Government called for a trial speed of 17 1/2 knots and a sea speed of 16 knots. The Canadian Pacific decided to exceed these requirements, and asked the builders to guarantee a speed of 18 knots on trial and 16 1/2 knots at sea. The most important mechanical feature of the *Empresses* was the provision of two independent triple-expansion engines, each driving a separate propellor. Though a commonplace these many years, twin screws were still a novelty in 1889, and the pioneer twin-screw Atlantic liner had only been in service for little more than a year. On the Pacific, even the new Pacific Mail liner *China*, which had just been delivered by the Fairfield Company, had only a single screw, and the *Empresses* were the only twin-screw steamers in the trans-Pacific trade for eight or nine years. On the long run to the Orient, in relatively unfrequented waters and long before the days of wireless, the duplication of machinery was an important safeguard against disaster, for a disabled steamer might drift helplessly for weeks without sighting another vessel.

The accommodation provided for first-class passengers compared well with that in the finest Atlantic liners of the day. During their early years in service the most advertised feature of the *Empresses* seems to have been the promenade-deck, which had a length of 220 feet. The contract called for a cargo capacity of 3,250 tons, in measurement tons of 40 cubic feet.

A tradition persists that the *Empresses* caused a great stir when they were being built, but there is little or no evidence to support the story. A careful search through several technical journals has failed to reveal even a detailed description of the vessels. There is no avoiding the fact that the failure of the *City of Rome* had cast a shadow over the Barrow shipyard which it took Bryce Douglas and the Naval Construction Company some years to dispel, and in reality the *Empresses* caused a sensation, not by their construction, but by their outstanding and consistent performance in service.

The cost of the three steamers, as given in the annual reports of the Canadian Pacific Railway, was $3,471,587, or slightly more than $1,157,000 each. According to reports current when she entered service, the cost of the Pacific Mail steamer *China* was only $826,000. As this comparison indicates, no reasonable expense was spared to make the *Empresses* fully capable of maintaining the service contemplated; and another of those intangible traditions, which are so difficult to prove or disprove, would have us believe that the Naval Construction Company was so anxious to deliver three ships of the first quality, and thereby enhance its reputation, that it lost money on the contract.[6]

The keel of the first of the steamers, the *Empress of India*, was laid in November, 1889, and she was launched only nine months later, on August 30, 1890. The christening ceremony was performed by Lady Louise Egerton, daughter of the chairman of the Naval Construction Company. David Jones, Assistant Archivist of C.P. Rail, has discovered that the names of the ships had been chosen a scant two months before the launching. Not long after the contract for their construction had been signed in 1889, H. Maitland Kersey, chief liaison between builders and owners, had suggested that the ships be named *Manchuria*, *Mongolia* and *Tiara*, with *Formosa* and *Corea* kept in mind for future additions to the fleet. (Three of these names were used later by the rival Pacific Mail.) Van Horne countered with a proposal to name the ships after Chinese dynasties, such as *Tai Cho*, *Tai Ming* and *Tai Ching*. Kersey objected strongly, as he felt this would not be well received in China, and that it would be prudent to use the names of Chinese rivers or towns instead. Finally, in June 1890, Van Horne informed Shaughnessy that R.B. Angus, a director of the C.P.R., had suggested the names *Empress of India*, *Empress of Japan* and *Empress of China*. Van Horne's comment was: "think very good. We can use *Empress of Russia*, *Germany* and *Austria* for additional ships." Kersey was unhappy; he thought such long names would be "a terrible nuisance. They take a lot of room in newspaper columns and it is a painful undertaking writing all this on bills-of-lading, documents, etc. I think shorter names would have been much better." Happily the *Empress* choice was adhered to.

Another matter settled very late in the day was the colour of the ships hulls. Then as now, models of ships were sent out for publicity purposes, and Kersey had three built with different coloured hulls — black, ivory-white and French grey. Grey seems never to have been seriously in the running, and Kersey's decision in favour of ivory-white came as the result of a long talk with Admiral Morant, who had had experience in ship maintenance when stationed at Hong Kong. Surprisingly, the Admiral contended that ivory-white hulls would be easier to maintain than black ones.

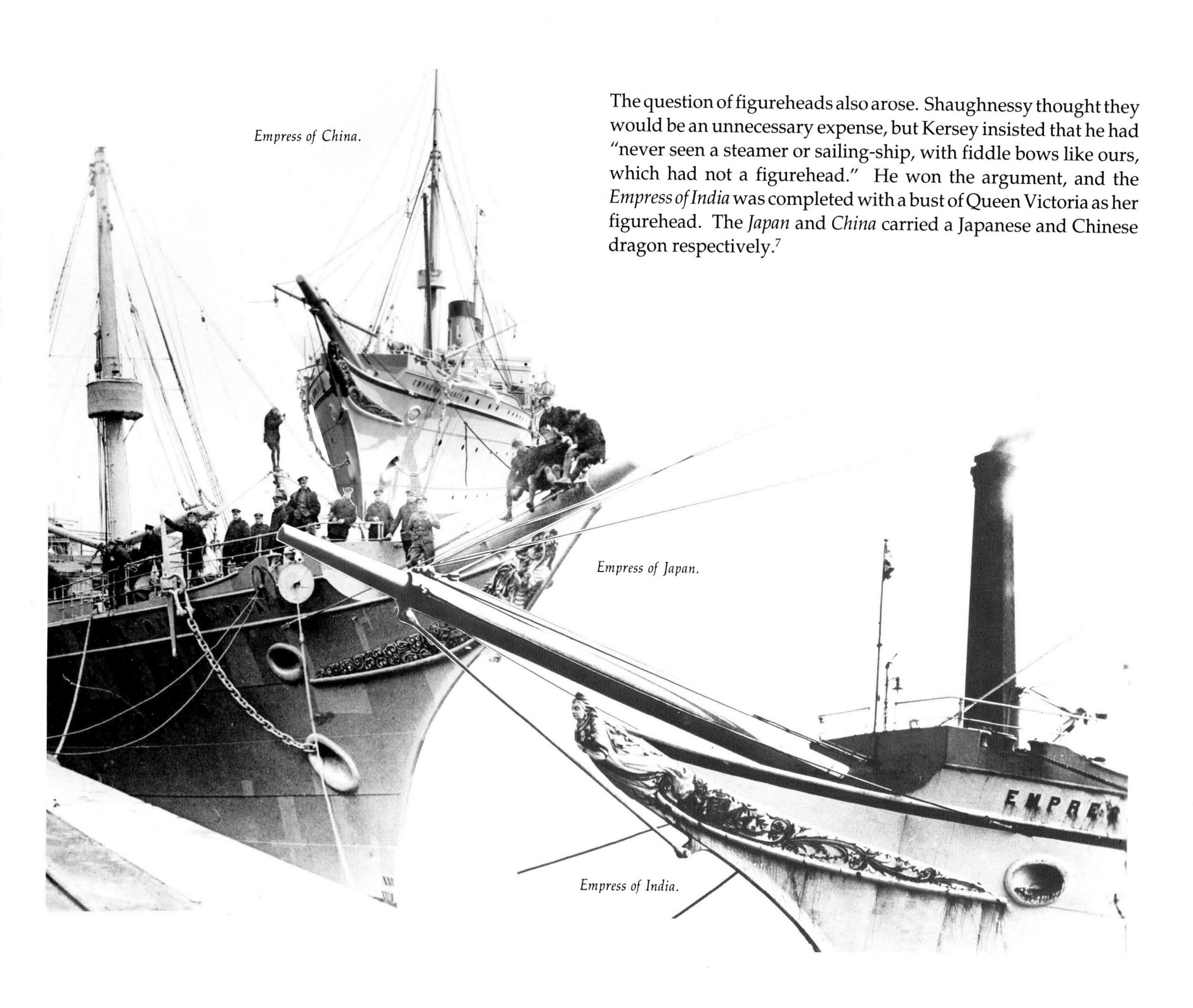

Empress of China.

The question of figureheads also arose. Shaughnessy thought they would be an unnecessary expense, but Kersey insisted that he had "never seen a steamer or sailing-ship, with fiddle bows like ours, which had not a figurehead." He won the argument, and the *Empress of India* was completed with a bust of Queen Victoria as her figurehead. The *Japan* and *China* carried a Japanese and Chinese dragon respectively.[7]

Empress of Japan.

Empress of India.

One of the models was on display in New York in December 1890.[8] The one with the black hull came to the Canadian Pacific offices in Montreal. In a letter to the writer Mr. M. McD. Duff recalled that the hull "was changed from black to white right behind the desk at which I worked during the Winter of 1892 and 1893."[9]

It was expected that the *Empress of India* would be completed in record time in another two months, but labour troubles intervened and she did not run her trials until January, 1891. Her fastest mean speed on the measured mile was 18.65 knots, which was comfortably in excess of the contract requirements. It is interesting to note that the trial trip of the *Empress of India* was the first occasion upon which the red and white checker-board house-flag of the Canadian Pacific was ever hoisted. The flag was designed by Van Horne, and its origin is described in an amusing letter to Mr. M. McD. Duff, Assistant to the Chairman, Canadian Pacific Steamships. Van Horne wrote:

> **Yes, I designed the house flag — partly to differ from any in use and partly that it might be easily recognized when hanging loose. It has no historical or heraldic significance. Somebody has suggested that it meant "three of a kind" but that would not be a big enough hand for the C.P.R. for which a "straight flush" only would be appropriate.**[10]

The second of the three ships, the *Empress of Japan*, was launched on December 13, 1890, by Lady Alice Stanley, daughter-in-law of Lord Stanley, then Governor-General of Canada.[11] The *Japan* was ready for her trials in March and proved to be slightly faster than the *Empress of India*. Her speed on the measured mile was 18.91 knots, and on a 500-mile sea trial she made the very satisfactory average speed of 16.85 knots.[12]

Empress of Japan (1) on her measured mile.

Meanwhile the *Empress of India* had sailed for the Far East, by way of the Mediterranean, to take up her station in the trans-Pacific service. For some months the Canadian Pacific had been advertising world tours in connection with the maiden voyages of the *Empresses*, and undertook to carry passengers "around the world in 80 days for $600." This was the nearest approach to a world cruise which had yet been offered; and the *Empress of India* had more than a hundred saloon passengers on board when she left Liverpool on February 8, 1891.

Empress of India : Captain Marshall, R.N.R. and officers, April, 1891.

She sailed under the command of Captain O.P. Marshall, late of the P. & O. Line, who became an Elder Brother of Trinity in later years and who died in 1939 at the age of 82. Her Chief Officer was Rupert Archibald, who later commanded the *Empress of China* for almost twenty years, and E.G. Montserrat sailed as Second Officer. The Chief Engineer was F.W. Wood, James Adamson was Second Engineer, and James E. Macrae, Purser.

Mr. Macrae, who had been Purser of the old *Abyssinia* in 1888-1890, recalls the following details of the voyage of the *Empress of India* from Liverpool to Hong Kong:

> We called at Gibraltar, where we spent the day, at Marseilles, where we spent three days, at Naples one day, then over to Port Said. I always remember the distance from Naples to Port Said — 1111 miles. We coaled at Port Said and our passengers were sent by train to Cairo and the Pyramids and rejoined us after we had made the passage of the canal, at Suez. From there we went direct to Colombo, Ceylon, passing near enough to Aden one forenoon to get a close-up view of the town and shipping. We were three days in Colombo, while some of the passengers went to Kandy, and I have recollections of a cricket match I attended, played by a team of our passengers, some of whom were members of the M.C.C., against Colombo. We lost, but a good time was enjoyed by all. After Colombo the next stop was Penang, where we spent a day, and then Singapore. We were specially favoured in the Straits for in one day we saw no less than four waterspouts at one time, and passed a fight between a killer and a whale. [probably a killer whale and a baleen whale.]
>
> After two days at Singapore we sailed for Hong Kong. We were scheduled to arrive at Hong Kong on March 16th at 1 p.m. and with true C.P.R. punctuality we threw out our first line to the Kowloon Wharf exactly as the clock struck one. I was in the corner of the bridge with Captain Marshall all the way in as I was the only officer who had been in Hong Kong before. We picked up our Chinese pilot outside Green Island Passage and he was very proud to take our lovely great white ship across the harbour, at the highest speed Captain Marshall would allow, with all our flags flying. We had a great reception, every steam whistle in the harbour was blowing to welcome us.

Purser: J.E.Macrae

Before Macrae left the *Abyssinia* he had been waited upon by the entire Chinese crew, to whom he had become much attached, and they had exacted from him a promise that he would take them with him on "the big new ship." The sequel appears in a further passage from his description of the arrival of the *Empress* at Hong Kong:

> On the Kowloon Wharf stood a long line of Chinese, drawn up like soldiers on parade, and as we came alongside they began waving to me, calling "Maclae, Maclae!" Captain Marshall said to me, "Who are your friends?" To which I answered very happily, "That's your new crew." It was the entire crew of the *Abyssinia*, paid off two weeks earlier, and they had not forgotten my promise made nine months before in Vancouver.[13]

At Hong Kong the *Empress* was dry-docked and painted, and many of her passengers travelled on to Japan and rejoined her later at a port of call there. She sailed finally on April 7, 1891 — the date which marked both the commencement of the regular *Empress* line service, and the start of the ten-year mail contract with the Canadian and British Governments. After calling at Shanghai, Nagasaki and Kobe, she left Yokohama on April 17, at 4:14 p.m., and at 6:30 a.m. on the 28th she dropped anchor off Victoria, where she was welcomed officially by Mayor Grant. Her total steaming-time from Hong Kong was 416 hours 33 minutes, and her average speed 15.16 knots. Though it was soon lowered both by herself and by her sister ships, her passage of 11 days 7 hours and 27 minutes from Yokohama was a land-to-land record, and she therefore ended her maiden voyage Queen of the Pacific.

The whole trip from Liverpool had been remarkably free from trouble. A heated low-pressure eccentric made it necessary to stop the port engine for a few hours between Hong Kong and Shanghai, but her twin screws enabled her to proceed at reduced speed and the main engines gave no further trouble. The refrigerator machinery failed in the heat between Suez and Singapore — a misfortune which befell each of the three *Empresses* in turn — but it proved equal to its task when the vessel reached the more temperate climate of her regular run. The most serious trouble experienced by the *Empresses* arose from their electric wiring, which proved to be insufficiently protected from wear and moisture. Electricity was still in its pioneer stage aboard ship in 1891, and this difficulty was to culminate, as we shall see, in a serious fire in the *Empress of Japan*.[14]

The *Empress of India* remained three hours at Victoria and then proceeded to Vancouver, where an elaborate welcome awaited her. Van Horne and a party of Canadian Pacific directors were on the dock, as well as Mayor Oppenheimer and other civic dignitaries. A grand banquet and ball were held in the evening at Hotel Vancouver, but Van Horne, who heartily disliked functions of the kind, left for Montreal in the afternoon. Fortunately the Hon. Edward Blake was in the city, and could assume the role of guest of honour.[15]

On this maiden voyage the *Empress* brought 131 saloon passengers and 355 Chinese in the steerage. Her cargo totalled 1,810 tons measurement, and consisted mostly of tea, silk, rice and opium.[16] Many of the saloon passengers and the through mail from the Orient, which consisted of twenty-seven bags, left for the East on a special train at 6:10 p.m. Just fifteen days later, on May 13, part of this mail was distributed in London, having been in transit only twenty-six days from Yokohama and thirty-six days from Hong Kong. This fact was reported in the British House of Commons by the Postmaster-General, who added that the last mail received from the Far East via Suez had been forty-five days in transit from Yokohama but only thirty-three days from Hong Kong.[17] As this indicates, the new service brought about an important saving of time for mails from Japan, but not from points in China beyond Shanghai.

Empress of India, 1891.

The *Empress of India* arrived in Vancouver with a double crew in certain departments, as Chinese stewards and firemen had been signed on at Hong Kong to replace the temporary English staff engaged at Liverpool for the voyage to the Far East. J.E. Macrae recalls that one of his first jobs when the vessel docked was to send this English staff off to Montreal, on their way home. He adds:

> **The firemen were about the roughest crowd that ever sailed out of Liverpool. Two Colonist cars were reserved for them on the train. Before they left the station in Vancouver they had smashed every piece of glass in the windows, and I heard later that when the cars reached Montreal their fittings had been entirely demolished by this tough gang.**

The *Empress of India* sailed from Vancouver on her first outward voyage on May 9, 1891, and arrived at Hong Kong on the 28th. Her average speed on the entire passage was 15.55 knots. She remained at Hong Kong for more than a month, partly to allow numerous small adjustments and alterations to be made and partly to let the *Empress of Japan* take her place in the trans-Pacific schedule.

The *Japan* had left Liverpool on April 11, and although her main engines gave great satisfaction minor troubles made part of the voyage to Hong Kong anything but enjoyable for J.N.L. Roberts, her harassed Purser. Between Suez and Colombo her refrigerator machinery failed, and to make matters worse her electric fans were continually breaking down. Finally, Roberts had to struggle with a staff which he considered incompetent. His report states that complaints were numerous, and that for a time "the grumbling was horrible"; but when the ship reached her station, and secured her experienced Chinese crew, things smoothed out rapidly. Her maiden trip across the Pacific proved to be both fast and pleasant, and she arrived at Victoria late in the evening on June 22, after a passage of 10 days 21 hours and 23 minutes from Yokohama. She brought 145 saloon, 4 second class, and 352 steerage passengers, or a total of 501 passengers in all, and her cargo totalled 2,318 tons measurement.[18]

Empress of Japan (1), Captain, officers and crew, 1898.

Empress of China News

No. 1.   **JULY 29, 1891.**

OFFICERS AND CREW.

CAPTAIN . . . . . ALEXANDER TILLETT.

Chief Officer	Mr H Pybas	Chief Engineer	Mr J Fowler
Second "	Mr Kysh	Second "	J McInnes
Third "	Mr Bowles	Third Engineer	E Murray
Fourth "	Mr Bellew	Fourth "	S Roberts
Doctor	Dr G S Meadows	Fifth "	H Hamilton
Purser	H L Coulson	Sixth "	J Heath
Carpenter	T Ley	Seventh "	W Pettigrew
Boatswain	F Lavery	Eighth "	W Farne
	R Tucker and T Johnson	Ninth "	G Monks
Master-at-Arms	J Gibbs	Tenth "	G Craig
Joiner	N Sinclair	Boilermaker	J Hibbert
Armourer	W Hill	Electrician	H Bonner
Quartermasters—	G Urquhart, W Norton,	Chief Steward	Mr D C Bisset
	J Wilson, J Quinn	Second "	A L Golden
Signalmen—		Stewardess	Miss O Walters
	H Pink and W Beveridge	Storekeeper	R Crichton
Lamptrimmer	W Jones	Barkeeper	H Williams
		Chef	W Wilson
Barber	Oscar Hyland	Baker	T Evans
Printer	D. W. Hutchison	Butcher	A Thomas

Sailing Department............ 50
Engineer Department......... 72
Steward Department.......... 48

Total Crew...... 170

PASSENGER LIST.

M Churchill, Zanesville, Ohio, USA
Miss Cumisky, Ballriggan, Ireland,
J H Curtis, Newhaven, Herrisburg, USA
John E Fox, Gloucester, England,
S H Fox, "
N Hamilton, Pennsylvania, USA,
John Harrison, Nicaragua,
G C Henry, Burlington, Iowa,
J A Marshall, Montreal,
John N Luning, San Francisco,
L W Lynch, Harrisburg, Pa,
Thornton N Motley, New York,
Dr F W Payne, Boston,
Miss Pritt, Zanesville, Ohio, USA,
Victor Robertson, St Paul, Minn.,
F Sawyer, Boston, USA,
J S Seaton, Manchester,
Rev E Urquhart, Devonshire,
E W Walker, London,
Wm F Warden, Paris,

TO OUR READERS.

The "NEWS" is an attempt to collect in a compact form a series of facts relating to our voyage and to amuse our passengers, both old and young. As a reference it should prove invaluable and is the best souvenir of the trip that you could send home. We intend publishing weekly and respectfully invite our passengers to contribute short articles or stories. No matter of a personal character will be entertained.

THE EMPRESS OF CHINA NEWS.

DIVINE SERVICE.

Divine service was held in the saloon on Sunday at 11 A. M. The service was conducted by Captain A. Tillett, assisted by Chief Officer H. Pybus.

OUR CANINE PASSENGERS.

Under the care of Butcher Thomas are a couple of handsome retriever dogs. Since their arrival on board they have become most popular pets, and it is amusing to note the manner in which they recognize their keeper. Good old "sea dogs."

MUSICAL MARINERS.

The boy sailors of the "Empress" are hard at work in their preparation of their programme of music with which they intend amusing us a little later on in the voyage. The band is composed of five, namely—J. Wood, T. Gilham, W. Green, W. Harris, and F. Cole, under the tutorship of Dr. G. S. Meadows.

ON DECK.

A game of baseball is on the tapis.

Football is all the rage. However, some difficulty is found in procuring a team able to tackle Old Sol's Arabians.

The crew on Saturday were mustered and put through fire and boat drill. On Sunday they were inspected by Captain A. Tillett.

The cricket season opened on board the 'Empress' last Thursday. The cricket ball used is a new departure, being on the principle of the Australian boomerang, returning to the bowler.

The race for the Empress of China Plate will take place some time next month. A big field is sure to face the starter. Bos'un may win, while Dog Watch should get a place.

Our next number will contain a full account of everything which may occur worth note. We are daily expecting the arrival of our famous carrier pigeons, who convey a most important message from the French capital.

ADVERTISEMENTS

BOY—Wanted, a smart lad to peel onions. Eyes must not water. Apply to Vegetable Cook.

YOUTH—A fine opening for a smart Youth. Apply, with references, at the down town branch of this paper.

WANTED—Boys to sell the "NEWS." Must be "hustlers" and come well recommended. Apply General Manager, Empress of China News.

PHOTOGRAPHY—Photographs of R.M.S. Empress of China may be obtained from the ship's Barber.

HAIRDRESSING—Oscar Hyland, Tonsorial Artist, No. 1 Midship Avenue, has all the latest improvements in nautical hairdressing, toilet equipments, fine hosiery, etc.

NAUTICAL PRINTING—Visiting cards, ball cards, etc., done on the shortest notice. Apply this office.

MUSIC—The Empress of China Band have a few open dates. Picnics and balls a specialty. Address Band Master, "News" Office.

NOTICE—A company is about to be formed for the purpose of running an 'L' road between Promenade Avenue and Turtle Back Park. Information and prospectus may be had from D. H. "News" Office.

SKATES—A large stock always on hand. Apply Ship's Cook's Mate.

BATHING—Lessons in swimming and floating given by Prof. Fat. Terms moderate. Aquarium.

Printed and published at the printing office of DAVID W. HUTCHISON, R. M. S. Empress of China.

First issue of the on-board newspaper of *Empress of China*; front and back pages. Collection: Vancouver Maritime Museum.

THE EMPRESS OF CHINA NEWS.

R.M.S. "EMPRESS OF CHINA."

The "Empress of China," built by the Naval Construction and Armament Company, Barrow-in-Furness, was launched on the 25th of March, 1891. Her dimensions are as follows:—Length over all, 496 feet; length between perpendiculars, 440 feet; breadth, moulded, 51 feet; depth, 36 feet, with 10 water tight compartments; gross tonnage, 5,700; horse power, 10,000. She is built of Siemen-Martin steel throughout, under Lloyd's special survey, and is classed 100 A1. She has special appliances to secure safety and is so divided that if any two compartments be filled with water (cargo and coal being in said compartments) the ship will not sink or be in an unmanageable condition. The engines are in two sets, driving twin screws, with longitudinal bulkhead, in which self-closing water tight doors are fitted between. Her coal capacity is 2,200 tons. She is fitted with gun platforms on the turtle deck, forward and aft, and has four gun stations on promenade deck and four gun stations on upper deck, to conform to the requirements of the British Admiralty, so that she may be speedily converted into an armed cruiser or troopship. Her speed on her trial trip was 18 knots. Funnels, cream colour. House flag, red and white squares.

OUR PORTS OF CALL.

The following are our ports of call:—Gibralter, Naples, Port Said, Suez, Colombo, Penang, Singapore, Hong Kong, Woosung, Yokohama, and our destination, Vancouver.

DOINGS ON THE 'CHANGE.

PORT STREET, Mid-day.—The market opened strong, Fans and Ice being in great demand. A cold chill struck the bears and the lambs seemed steady. Sardines seemed a glut on the market, while Hot Rolls are on the decline and Bread on the rise. Canadian Pacific Railroad stock and shares in British Columbia are eagerly asked for. "Empress of China" (preferred) still remains steady.

A CRY UNHEARD ON BOARD THE "EMPRESS."

"Stew—Stew—ar—d! I am—going—to be——hic——!"

A NOVEL EXPEDITION.

On Dit, That a party will leave the Smoking Room to-day at 3 P. M., via baloon, for the maintop, where a certain gentleman will endeavour to rob the "Crow's Nest." We wish him luck.

THE MIKADO'S VISIT.

Hong Kong, July 28—Reports here say that the great Mikado intends paying a visit to the "Empress of China" on her arrival.

LATEST NEWS.
(BY SPECIAL CABLE TO THE "NEWS.")

New York, July 28.—Great interest is centred here concerning the welfare of the "Empress of China." Reports have arrived here to the effect that the impregnable rock of Gibralter had been taken by the "Empress" and towed up to Naples, where an immense derrick is being erected for the purpose of lifting the rock and dropping it down the burning volcano of Vesuvius.

LATER.—A piece of the rock of Gibralter was sold to-day for the sum of £50.

THE EMPRESS OF CHINA NEWS.

OUR WEATHER FORECAST.
(BY THE MAN ALOFT.)

Special message from Old Sol says overcoats will be necessary after leaving Suez. Slight showers of roasted snowballs will prevail on Friday, followed by sleet and rain. On Saturday skating may be enjoyed on the Turtle Pond. Sunday, Clerk of Weather will visit in person.

DAILY RUNS.

Wednesday, July 15, 4 P. M., left Liverpool.
Thursday, July 16 . . . . . 278½ miles
Friday, July 17 . . . . . 315½ miles
Saturday, July 18 . . . . . 347 miles
Sunday, July 19, Gibraltar, . . 297½ miles
Monday, July 20 . . . . . 184 miles
Tuesday, July 21 . . . . . 284 miles
Wednesday, July 22 . . . . . 257 miles
Thursday, July 23, Naples . . 250½ miles
Friday, July 24 . . . . . 231 miles
Saturday, July 25 . . . . . 316 miles
Sunday, July 26 . . . . . 319 miles
Monday, July 27, Port Said . . 240 miles
Tuesday, July 28, Port Said to Suez 88 miles
Wednesday, July 29 . . . . . 182.7 miles

ACROSTIC ON OUR CAPTAIN'S NAME.

A fine young ship, with a gallant crew,
Left the Mersey—this day, weeks two,
Endless regrets and sad farewells
Xtend their wail like the sea's dull swell.
Ah! cruel the parting for poor Jack Tar,
Nearest and dearest to leave thus far,
Dark'ning the home he had made so bright,
Eyes that to him shed nought but light,
Risking his life on the stormy main,
Toiling for those he mayn't see again.
In every weather, and in every clime,
List and you'll hear the sailor's chime,
Let their faults then be what they may,
Ever for our brave men we'll pray
That He who counts e'en the grains of sand
Take us all to Him to the better Land.

ANONYMOUS.

WHAT WE HAVE SEEN.

Since our departure from Liverpool on the 15th of July our passengers have been treated most kindly by King Neptune sea sickness being a thing unknown on board the Empress of China. We arrived at Gibraltar on Sunday morning, July 19, where most of our passengers went ashore. On resuming our way some of the prettiest skies adorned the firmament and our Special Artist has managed to portray one or two, which will be published later on. Naples, with its glorious Vesuvius, was reached on the 23rd, where the bum boat men plied their trade galore. On the 27th we arrived at Port Said, where, well, we had a coaling seige. White muslins and white clothing had a hard time. The cry of the sons of the desert still rings in our ears. "Ali! Allah! Allah! Goola!" After wending our way through the Suez Canal, witnessing many interesting scenes of desert life, we arrived on Tuesday evening at Suez, and after a couple of hours' stay resumed our onward course. Our next stopping place is Colombo.

EDITOR.

Inner pages of the on-board newspaper.

The *Empress of Japan* was under the command of Captain George A. Lee, who was already well known on the Pacific as captain of the *Parthia*. The other interesting name in the list of officers is that of Edward Beetham, her Fourth Officer, of whom more will be heard later. Thomas Tod was Chief Engineer.

The *Empress of India* and *Empress of Japan* completed two round trips between Hong Kong and Vancouver before they were joined by the *Empress of China*. The last of the three pioneers was launched by Lady Northcote on March 25, 1891, and ran her trials early in July. For no apparent reason, for she was identical in design, she developed about 600 more horsepower than her sisters, and worked up to a full 19 knots on the measured mile.[19] Oddly enough, this initial performance was the best of her career, for on the regular run to the Orient she proved to be neither the fastest nor the most economical of the three ships.

The *Empress of China* sailed from Liverpool on July 15. In 1891 a world cruise still seemed to be a venturesome proposal, and the maiden voyages of the two other *Empresses* apparently exhausted its appeal. Only twenty-one saloon passengers sailed in the *China*, but they appear to have had a thoroughly good time. Each was berthed in a separate cabin, and the *Empress of China News,* a four-page paper, was printed on board each week for their amusement. At the end of the voyage H.L. Coulson, the Purser, was able to report that he had received no complaints whatsoever. Unfortunately, the trip was marred towards the end by very rough weather between Yokohama and Victoria, and 12 days 9 hours were spent on the passage. It was not until the morning of September 23 that she finally docked in Vancouver. For purposes of record it may be added that the *Empress of China* brought 67 saloon, 4 second class, and 104 steerage passengers; and her cargo, which consisted mostly of tea, measured 2,525 tons. Her list of officers contains several names of interest. Her commander, Captain A. Tillett, made only two round trips in her, as he was then promoted to the post of Marine Superintendent for the Canadian Pacific at Hong Kong. Her Chief Officer was Henry Pybus, and her Chief Engineer James Fowler, who, it will be remembered, had watched the construction of the engines of all three of the steamers at the shipyard.[20]

With the arrival of the *Empress of China* the last of the old chartered steamers was retired, and the three new sister ships began to shuttle back and forth across the Pacific with a regularity which was to become proverbial. In the course of years they established a record for adherence to schedule which has probably never been equalled on the seven seas. Though the mail contract called for only a twenty-eight-day service, the Canadian Pacific increased this to a departure every twenty-one days between April and September, which raised the number of sailings to fifteen per year. Yet for no less than fifteen years — from 1891 to 1906 — no *Empress* ever missed a sailing or was ever penalized for the late arrival of her mails.

There is no doubt that the foresight of the Canadian Pacific in ordering steamers which could exceed the trial speeds called for in the mail contract made this astonishing record possible. Upon innumerable occasions the task of getting the mails to Hong Kong on time resembled nothing so much as an obstacle race. Forty years ago the Atlantic steamer service to Canada left much to be desired, and the railway service across the Continent was both relatively slow and subject to delays of many kinds. It was quite usual for the English mails to reach Vancouver at least one day late, and of course an *Empress* could not sail until they arrived. Delays of two and even three days were not infrequent. In 1899 matters were improved greatly when the first "Imperial Limited" was put on the run in summer, and reduced the train journey from Montreal to 100 hours. But as late as July, 1902 — to quote only a single example — the *Empress of China* sailed from Vancouver more than 3 days and 2 hours behind schedule. Two days of this time was made up on the voyage to Yokohama, and another day was gained during a fast run from Shanghai to Hong Kong, where the *China* arrived just 7 hours and 37 minutes within her contract time.

Empress of China at Rithet's Wharf, Victoria.

The late arrival of the mails at Vancouver was only one of the many difficulties which had to be overcome in the never-ending endeavour to keep the *Empresses* on schedule. They were both carefully run and lucky ships, but nevertheless they had their share of small accidents. For example, the *Empress of Japan* bumped a rock when leaving Vancouver on her sixth voyage in 1892. A diver found that she had suffered only very slight damage to a propellor, but it had been necessary to hold her overnight at Victoria for examination.[21] Homeward bound, early in August, she found herself in much greater peril. When 800 miles from Yokohama her lights flickered and then went out, and it was discovered that the electric cables had fused in the after-hold and caused a fire there. Efforts to check the flames proved unavailing, so with hatches battened down she turned about and headed at full speed for Hakodate. When the fire had been extinguished and the damage repaired she set sail once more for Vancouver. Though she arrived laden to the hatches and found a large outward cargo awaiting her, she was prepared for sea in only six days and left for the Orient on time.[22] Some two years later, in August, 1894, the *Empress of China* suffered a serious delay from another cause, when the incompetence of a pretended pilot stranded her on the Woosung spit, and she remained ashore for nine days.[23] All three *Empresses* collided with junks at various times, but it remained for the *Empress of Japan* to ram a whale with such violence that she had to go hard astern to get clear.[24]

Storms played their part in the lives of the *Empresses*. The *Empress of India* was the first of the trio to encounter a typhoon, but it scarcely matched in violence the tempestuous weather encountered by the *Empress of China* on her second passage from Yokohama to Vancouver. The gale persisted for seven days; and at the height of the storm the hurricane-deck shipped water, which poured through the fiddle-gratings and fell into the stoke-hole. Movables on deck were carried away and a steel lifeboat stove in. This second round voyage had been a trying time for the officers of the *China*, for on the outward passage she met headwinds so continuously that she was compelled to put in at Hakodate for coal; one of her seamen was killed in a fall at Hong Kong, and when she finally reached Vancouver a case of smallpox was found aboard and she had to raise steam hastily and return to the quarantine station at Albert Head.[25] But through all these misfortunes the *Empress* ploughed her way, and succeeded in keeping herself approximately on schedule and her mails on time.

The *Empress of China* enjoyed no monopoly of bad weather. In 1895 the *Empress of India* had her bridge disabled in a storm, and in March, 1898, it was in great part carried away in what was perhaps the most severe gale she ever encountered. The *Empress of Japan* came through a typhoon in October, 1899, when two days out of Yokohama, which not only stove in several of her boats but smashed the smoking-room skylight and flooded the room and a number of cabins.

Mention has been made of smallpox, and it should be added that both smallpox and, upon occasion, the plague broke out amongst the steerage passengers and threatened to delay the liners. Every care was taken to keep the steerage isolated, and the consequence was that saloon passengers very rarely suffered much inconvenience or detention at quarantine. Much the most serious delay was caused in June, 1901, when the *Empress of China* — which deserves to rank as the unlucky one amongst the three pioneers — was held at Nagasaki for ten days following an outbreak of plague in the steerage. An epidemic was raging in the Orient at the time, and as a precautionary measure the *Empresses* ceased to carry Asiatic passengers for several months. It should be added that, following her experience at Nagasaki, the *Empress of China* averaged 16.6 knots on the passage to Vancouver, managed to arrive only eight days late, contrived to prepare for sea in only five days, and sailed on the return passage on time.

Lastly, the *Empresses* managed to keep to schedule despite wars and rumours of wars. The impression that the years previous to 1914 were peaceful is largely illusory; and it is interesting to recall that during the years 1891-1906, when the *Empresses* were setting up their record, no less than four major conflicts troubled the Far East — the Sino-Japanese War, which broke out in 1894; the Spanish-American War, which commenced in 1898; the Boxer Rebellion of 1900; and the Russo-Japanese War, which was declared early in 1904.

From the first the *Empress of Japan* proved to be a little faster than her sisters, and her maiden passage from Yokohama to Victoria, which she made in 10 days 21 hours and 23 minutes, took the trans-Pacific record from the *Empress of India* by a margin of more than ten hours. When she returned to Hong Kong she was dry-docked, and on August 11, fresh from overhaul, she sailed for Vancouver on what was to prove a memorable voyage. Though no document has come to light which so states, there is every reason to believe that she sailed with orders to make the best time she could, consistent with safety and reasonable economy.

She responded by travelling from Hong Kong to Vancouver in a total steaming-time of only 380 hours, at an average speed of 16.31 knots. Trans-Pacific records are timed between Yokohama and the Pacific Coast, and the *Empress* made her best time on this leg of the journey. Clipping more than eight hours off her previous run, she arrived in the Royal Roads only 10 days 13 hours and 10 minutes from Yokohama, with an average speed of 16.59 knots to her credit.

This record run gave the Canadian Pacific an opportunity which it seized with alacrity. The *Empress of Japan* reached the Royal Roads early on the morning of August 29, 1891. She hurried on to Vancouver, and a special train left for the East with her mails at 1 p.m. The 2,803 miles to Brockville, Ontario, were covered at an average speed of 36.3 miles per hour, and with the co-operation of Canadian and United States postal officials the mails were quickly transferred across the river to Morristown and rushed on to New York. The end of the story contains the most dramatic touch of all, for the train bearing the mails reached the Grand Central Station on September 2, at 4:43 a.m., just seventeen minutes before the express steamer *City of New York* was due to sail for Liverpool. She obligingly waited a few minutes, and at 5:10 cast off her lines with letters on board which had left Yokohama only fifteen days before. Rising to the occasion, she made a fast passage across the Atlantic, and the mails reached London at 10:12 a.m. on September 9, only twenty-two days from Yokohama. Their arrival aroused great interest on both sides of the Atlantic, and did much to establish the reputation of the new *Empress* line.[26]

Some years later the *Empress of Japan* further reduced her time for the passage from Yokohama to Victoria to 10 days 10 hours, and this record stood until the arrival of the new *Empress of Russia* in 1913.

Meanwhile, in 1897, she had set up a westbound record which was never approached by either of her sisters. This fast run was occasioned by a delay in the arrival of the English mails, which reached Vancouver no less than five days late. Instead of sailing on schedule on June 21, the *Empress* did not get away from Victoria until 4:10 p.m. on the 26th. Captain Lee was on leave at the time and she sailed under the command of Captain Henry Pybus, who was instructed to make every effort to reach Hong Kong within the contract time. The engine- and boiler-room staffs, under Chief Engineer E.O. Murphy, responded magnificently, and the *Japan* arrived at Yokohama at 1:35 p.m. on July 7, after a passage of only 10 days 3 hours and 39 minutes.

Her average speed was 17.14 knots, and on July 1 she had set up a record run for a single day of 441 miles, at an average speed of 18.4 knots.[27] In addition to lowering the record, this phenomenal run enabled the *Empress* to catch up on her schedule and deliver her mails in Hong Kong on time.

Though the *Empress of Japan* never lost the blue ribbon, her sisters both exceeded an average speed of 16.5 knots on the trans-Pacific run, and they, too, had their moments in the limelight. One of these came the way of the *Empress of India* in 1896, when she was popularly credited with having won a race with the United States cruiser *Olympia*.

Captain Henry Pybus.

U.S.S. Olympia.

It is difficult at this late date to get to the bottom of the story, but the facts appear to be as follows:

The *Olympia* was a cruiser of 5,870 tons displacement, and when completed in 1894 she attained a speed of 21.69 knots on trial. In January, 1896, she was in Japanese waters, supposedly with the object of demonstrating her speed and efficiency, with a view to securing orders for warships from Japan for American shipyards. Late in the month she arrived at Kobe, and a story went the rounds that she had recently maintained a speed of 22 knots through a heavy gale and was about to attempt a record passage from Kobe to Nagasaki in order to prove her capabilities.

At this point the *Empress of India* entered the picture. She was engaged in the familiar task of making up time with her English mails, and was therefore running on a faster schedule than usual. About 5 p.m. on January 22 the *Olympia* left Kobe, bound for Nagasaki. At 9:25 p.m. the *Empress of India*, which had been in port most of the day, left for the same destination. The next day, in beautiful weather, the *Empress* slowly overhauled and passed the cruiser, and her log was endorsed: "Passed United States Warship *Olympia* at Simonesaki." Her log shows further that her average speed on the whole 390 miles from Kobe to Nagasaki was 16.64 knots.

It seems perfectly clear that nothing in the nature of a race really took place. It is possible that in view of the excitement amongst his passengers, which contemporary accounts show was intense, Captain Pybus, who happened to be in command of the *India* that trip, kept the *Empress* up to her comfortable full speed, but there is no reason to suppose that the *Olympia* could not have outdistanced her if she had tried. Be that as it may, the wide publicity given to the incident certainly added to the prestige of the *Empress* liners.[28]

It should be understood that the voyages with which we have been dealing were quite exceptional. They were made at relatively high speeds, either to establish the reputation of the line or to fulfil the requirements of the mail contract. The average trans-Pacific crossing was made at a much more modest rate.

In 1899 an attempt was made in certain quarters to discredit the northern route to the Orient from British Columbia, as compared with that from San Francisco. It was contended that the route to the north was so beset by fog and smoke that the vessels plying upon it derived no advantage from the fact that it was many miles shorter. T.G. Shaughnessy considered that this criticism merited serious consideration, and therefore released the following very interesting table giving the average length of the voyages of the *Empresses* over a period of four years:

AVERAGE LENGTH OF PASSAGE, YOKOHAMA TO VICTORIA.

Year	Westbound Hours	Minutes	Eastbound Hours	Minutes
1895	303	41	285	16
1896	303	30	289	32
1897	298	36	287	44
1898	302	32	287	16

Shaughnessy added that these figures covered an average of fifteen round voyages per annum, and stated that the *Empress* schedule called for an average speed of 14.5 knots westbound and 15 knots eastbound. He next examined the sailing lists of the three trans-Pacific lines operating out of San Francisco, and showed that their scheduled time on the voyage to Yokohama, via Honolulu, was 439 hours westbound and 363 hours eastbound. The equivalent time on a direct run from San Francisco to Yokohama would be 425 hours and 351 hours respectively. A simple calculation revealed that to cover the distance in the time stated a vessel would only have to average 12.5 knots on the passage to Yokohama and 12.9 knots on the return voyage.[29]

In a word, Shaughnessy was able to prove, beyond any doubt, that the *Empresses* were not only scheduled to run at a higher speed on their shorter route than the San Francisco steamers, but had maintained their scheduled speed with unfailing regularity for the previous four years.

2.

In the shipping world reputations are rarely made in a day, but fame and popularity seem to have come the way of the *Empresses* almost with their maiden voyages. No doubt this was due in part to the fact that they were the largest and fastest steamers trading across the Pacific. Even in 1891 size and speed made a strong appeal. But in addition, the graceful appearance of the vessels, and their very names, seem to have caught the imagination of the travelling public.

The consequence was that they immediately captured a large share of the first-class passenger trade. In 1890 the old chartered liners had landed 279 saloon passengers at Victoria and Vancouver. In 1892, the first complete year they were in service, the three *Empresses* landed 993.[30] In 1897 Van Horne could state that they were carrying "60 percent of all the first-class travel across the Pacific notwithstanding that there are 18 steamships competing for the business."

The traffic was seasonal. In April, May and June the *Empresses* almost always arrived with their saloon accommodation well filled. Outward voyages to the orient were busiest in September, October and November. The fluctuation in passenger lists in the course of the year was often startling. In 1897, for example, the number of first class passengers carried eastbound varied from 14 to 130. Four sailings in the rush season handled more than half the saloon passengers booked during the whole year.

Steerage travel fluctuated less violently. The chief seasonal influence was the Chinese New Year, to celebrate which many Celestials made a round trip to the Orient, thereby swelling westbound passenger lists just before, and eastbound lists just after, the great event. During the nineties most of the steerage passengers were Chinese. When the head tax imposed on Chinese immigrants entering Canada was increased from $50 to $100 in 1901, and finally to $500 at the beginning of 1904, this traffic was naturally affected, but substantial numbers continued to be carried. In later years many of the Oriental passengers were bound for distant destinations, notably the West Indies. In attracting this trade the *Empresses* benefited greatly from their close association with a transcontinental railway.

After the turn of the century the number of Japanese carried increased sharply, and in 1905 Hindu immigrants appeared on the passenger lists. The peak was reached in 1907 and 1908, when as many as 700 Hindus landed from a single ship. This trade ended abruptly when a "gentleman's agreement" was concluded with Japan, and steps were taken to bar Hindu immigration.

In view of the many factors involved, it is surprising that the total number of steerage passengers carried did not fluctuate more widely. In 1892 the eastbound total was 4,312. In 1897 it was 5,341, and it seems to have remained thereabouts for a good many years. In the six-year period 1908-13, for example, it averaged 5,630. Westbound steerage traffic in the same period averaged 3,690. The average total movement in both directions was thus 9,320.[32]

In November, 1891, T.G. (later Baron) Shaughnessy, then Vice-President of the Canadian Pacific, sailed from Vancouver in the *Empress of Japan* with instructions "to look into matters generally and to make such arrangements for conducting the company's business in China and Japan as he may find necessary."[33] This commission he carried out so effectively that the *Empresses* continued to sail with well-filled holds, even during the depression years of 1892-95.

Homeward-bound the most important items in their cargoes were silk and tea. Speed was of cardinal importance in the transport of raw silk, and, since they offered the fastest schedule, the *Empresses* captured a large proportion of this trade. Million-dollar shipments were carried from time to time. Even this figure was surpassed in 1902 when, within forty days, Canadian Pacific steamers landed four silk cargoes in Vancouver valued at $5,941,000.[34] Tea shipments came mostly from Japan. Extra ships were chartered occasionally at the peak of the season if more cargo was offered than the *Empresses* could handle. The sailing-vessels *J.B. Walker* and *Benjamin Sewell* landed 5,500 tons measurement of tea at Vancouver in 1891, and the steamer *Hupeh* made a voyage for the Company in 1896 and another in 1897.

Opium shipments arrived on almost every steamer for some years. Rice was also carried in large quantities. Curios and a small assortment of miscellaneous packages completed the usual inward cargoes on the *Empresses*.

For many years the most important items in their outward cargoes were flour and cotton goods. At first almost all the flour carried came from Portland, Oregon. Its usual destination was either China or New South Wales. The latter trade continued even after the establishment of a direct line of steamers between British Columbia and Australia, in 1893. Efforts were made later to develop a market for Canadian flour in Japan.[35] Other important cargo items were machinery and a variety of manufactured goods. In common with other lines, the Canadian Pacific found that the volume of freight loaded for the Orient was substantially lower, on the average, than that carried inward. Nevertheless the *Empresses* frequently sailed with capacity cargoes, and sometimes were even compelled to leave freight on the dock.

The annual reports of the Company show that even in 1891, when their reputations were still in the making, the three steamers "cleared their working expenses and the interest on their cost, without taking into account the value of the business contributed to the railway itself."[36] Shareholders were informed in the report for 1893 that the *Empresses* had "shown a healthy increase in profits each year since the line was established."[37] A year later the directors reported that these profits had risen by $80,467 in 1894, in spite of the prevailing depression.[38]

In 1895, though hard times continued, profits fell by only $3,000.[39] Though mentioned quite casually in the annual report, this fact was actually of vital importance to the Company, for it was the revenue derived from the *Empresses*, together with the through traffic they brought for the railway, which "helped to save the Canadian Pacific from the disaster which sunk a hundred and fifty-six American railroads in the depression of 1893-95 and might well have overwhelmed a new railway through Canada depending for its existence on local business."[40]

Freight traffic grew so rapidly that the Canadian Pacific was contemplating additions to its trans-Pacific fleet only two years after the *Empresses* were completed. "The experience of the Company in this trade indicates the need of a more frequent freight service," the report to the shareholders for 1893 stated, "and your authority will be asked for the building at the discretion of the Board and at such time as the general conditions of trade may warrant, two freight steamships to supplement the three passenger steamships now in the line."[41] The authority asked for was duly given, but the project was dropped, owing to the depression of 1893-95.

When reinforcements for the Pacific fleet finally arrived, they came from an unexpected quarter. The gold-rush to the Klondyke, which caused immense excitement in 1897, induced the Canadian Pacific to enter the coastal trade. Late in the year the Company purchased the steamers *Athenian* and *Tartar* from the old Union Line, and announced that they would be placed on the run from Vancouver to Skagway the following spring. Captain Archibald, commander of the *Empress of China*, was sent to England to bring out the *Tartar*, which sailed from Southampton on February 5, 1898. Travelling by way of Cape Horn, she arrived in Vancouver on April 1. Her cargo included a submarine telegraph cable which the *Tartar* herself laid between English Bay and Departure Bay — that is to say, between Vancouver and Nanaimo, on Vancouver Island — on April 6.[42] On the 12th the *Athenian* arrived, under the command of Captain H. Mowatt, formerly Second Officer of the *Empress of India*. Captain Mowatt remained in the *Athenian* for some years, but Captain Archibald resumed command of the *Empress of China* and was succeeded in the *Tartar* by Captain Henry Pybus.

The service to Skagway called for a departure every Thursday. The first sailing was taken by the *Tartar* on April 28, 1898. Unfortunately, it soon became apparent that traffic was quite insufficient to give profitable employment to such large steamers and they were withdrawn in July, after each vessel had made but six round voyages. The last trip of the *Tartar* is of interest because she arrived at Skagway just after the death of the notorious "Soapy" Smith. As a result she had the doubtful honour of carrying away his accomplices and henchmen, who were forced to flee the country.[43]

After swinging idly at anchor for several months in Vancouver Harbour, the *Athenian* and *Tartar* entered the trans-Pacific trade. The *Athenian* sailed in October for Vladivostock, carrying a heavy cargo which had been loaded at Portland. She was then laid up at Hong Kong for a time and did not return to Vancouver until April, 1899. After a trip to San Francisco she made a second voyage to the Orient, in the course of which she rode out a great storm at Kobe. Meanwhile, in December, the *Tartar* had entered service, and on her first homeward passage carried 600 Japanese to Hawaii. Her call at Honolulu was the first to be made there by a Canadian Pacific steamer. The *Tartar* made two more trips to the Orient, but both she and the *Athenian* were employed somewhat spasmodically, and no attempt was made to place them on a regular schedule or relate their sailings to those of the *Empresses*.

As early as June, 1898, when the Spanish-American war was in progress, the United States Government had wished to charter the *Athenian* and *Tartar* for its transport service. The offer had been refused because the Canadian Pacific would have preferred to sell the vessels at that time. Early in 1899 the United States found itself faced

Empress of Japan (1), painted window from Dining Saloon.
Collection: Mr. James M. Pearson.

Empress of Japan (1), painted window from Dining Saloon.
Collection: Mr. James M. Pearson.

with an insurrection in the Philippines, and a little later, when the offer of a charter was repeated, it was accepted by the Company. The *Tartar* was taken over for six months, as from July 4, 1899. This was later extended to nine months, and she was not turned back to her owners until April, 1900. The *Athenian* was chartered later in July, 1899, and served for a similar period. The vessels were employed in carrying troops, horses, and supplies from Pacific Coast ports to Manila. The *Athenian* proved so satisfactory, and Captain Mowatt was so popular with the United States Army officers, that she was taken over a second time in July, 1900, when the Boxer Rebellion made further troop movements necessary, and retained until February, 1901. These charters were in effect practically continuous, for in the brief interval between them she made a special voyage for the United States Army to St. Michael, Alaska.

Tartar, 1883.

Saloon Passenger list from the early days of the Trans-Pacific Service.
Collection: Vancouver Maritime Museum.

Athenian with her sails up!

The *Tartar* returned to the ordinary trans-Pacific trade in May of 1900, and was joined by the *Athenian* the following year. In the autumn of 1901 it was at last determined to operate the vessels on a regular schedule, and thus establish an intermediate service which would supplement the express service maintained by the *Empresses*. The first sailing was taken by the *Tartar* from Vancouver in September, 1901. Thereafter regular Canadian Pacific departures increased from fifteen to twenty-four or twenty-five per annum.

The *Tartar* and *Athenian* were not ideal additions to the trans-Pacific fleet, but they were soundly-built ships and useful traders. Moreover, their capital charges were low, as they had cost the Company no more than $297,000.[44] Both were iron, single-screw steamers, designed to run in the mail service of the Union Line between England and South Africa. The *Athenian* was of 3,882 tons gross, and was built at Whiteinch, near Glasgow, in 1882. The *Tartar* was a little larger, registered 4,425 tons, and came from the same yard in 1883.

For more than a decade the three orignal *Empresses* were beyond dispute the premier ships in the trans-Pacific trade. So far as saloon passengers were concerned, their only serious rival was the Fairfield-built Pacific Mail liner *China*, which sailed out of San Francisco. On the northern route the Upton Line, which attempted to establish a service from Portland to the Orient, soon collapsed, and for a time the only competition came from the old *Victoria* and *Tacoma* (formerly the *Parthia* and *Batavia*) and a few chartered steamers, all of which were sailing from Tacoma in connection with the Northern Pacific Railway. Though of little importance as competitors for the saloon trade, these vessels were popular with the Chinese, and in later years handled much more freight than the *Empresses*.

Presently a new and more aggressive rival appeared on the scene in the person of James J. Hill, President of the Great Northern Railway. In 1896 he concluded a working agreement with the Nippon Yusen Kaisha, which led to the establishment of the first Japanese steamer line across the Pacific. The pioneer ship of the service arrived in Seattle on August 31, and monthly sailings were maintained thereafter. In a few years the N.Y.K. was able to assign larger ships to the Seattle line, and by 1901 the vessels employed exceeded the *Empresses* in size. The *Kaga Maru*, for example, was of 6,301 tons gross, and when she reached Victoria on July 9, 1901, she was the largest ship which had ever used the port. But much more startling developments were in store, for by that date it was known that Hill was not satisfied with the improved N.Y.K. service. He was planning to organize a steamer line of his own, and to build and operate several monster ships of 20,000 tons in the trans-Pacific trade.

Meanwhile new rivals had appeared, or were in prospect, on the southern route. A second Japanese trans-Pacific line had been started by the Toyo Kisen Kaisha, and the company's first vessel, the *Nippon Maru*, arrived in San Francisco in January, 1899. She and her two sister ships slightly exceeded the Canadian Pacific liners in size, and imitated their appearance so obviously, with their twin funnels and clipper bows, that the crews of the Canadian ships immediately dubbed them the "tin *Empresses*." As they were operated on different routes, their relative capabilities were rarely put to a test, but the *Empresses* were undoubtedly superior in speed. The story goes that upon one occasion the *Nippon Maru* undertook to race the *Empress of India* between Oriental ports. Despite the fact that her boilers were forced to such an extent that she burned the paint off her funnels, she dropped far astern.[45] On the San Francisco run, however, the *Nippon Maru* and her sisters could outstrip any of their competitors, with the possible exception of the *China*. Fortunately for the Pacific Mail Company, its financial resources were sufficient to meet the situation, and before the end of 1899 it was able to order two new steamers, intended to be the largest and fastest on the Pacific.

In the midst of all this competition, actual or impending, the Canadian Pacific seems to have remained curiously unperturbed. When paying a visit to Vancouver in 1897 Van Horne told newspapermen that "trade and traffic" with the Orient were

outgrowing the present service. That service must be made more frequent and quicker, and we hope some day to be able to substitute larger steamships for the *Empresses* of the China line, and establish a fortnightly service...[46]

How soon this would be done, however, he could not say. Four years later, in August, 1901, action on the matter was evidently contemplated, as the directors reported that

The growth of the Company's traffic on the Pacific Ocean suggests the importance of providing at an early date an additional steamship, somewhat larger and faster than the [present] Pacific Steamships of the Company.[47]

The shareholders subsequently authorized the issue of bonds to cover the cost of construction, but no order for a new steamer was placed.

This left the three pioneer *Empresses*, supported after a fashion by the *Athenian* and *Tartar*, to meet the intense competition which now developed in the trans-Pacific trade. In July, 1902, the first of the new Pacific Mail liners, the *Korea*, entered service. On her second homeward voyage she sailed from Yokohama with orders to omit the usual call at Honolulu and to do her best to capture the Pacific record. She arrived in San Francisco on October 28, having covered 4,537 miles in only 10 days 15 hours and 15 minutes, at an average speed of 17.8 knots. So far as average speed was concerned this passage broke all records, as it surpassed the 17.14 knots which the *Empress of Japan* had maintained on her famous voyage in 1897. If the *Korea* had been travelling on the shorter northern route, she would, of course, have broken the time record as well. Even on a course 300 miles longer than that to Victoria, she was only 5 hours and 15 minutes behind the *Empress of Japan's* fastest homeward passage of 10 days 10 hours.

The *Korea* was joined by her sister ship, the *Siberia*, early in 1903. Together they cost the Pacific Mail Company almost $4,000,000.[48] The *Siberia* registered 11,284 tons gross — 8 tons more than the *Korea* — and by this narrow margin was the largest ship on the Pacific. She did not hold the distinction for long, for about the time she entered service the Pacific Mail purchased two still larger steamers, which were building for the trans-Atlantic trade, and renamed them *Manchuria* and *Mongolia*. They registered 13,639 tons gross and were completed in 1904. Within three years the Pacific Mail thus acquired four new liners totalling almost 50,000 tons, the average size of which was more than twice that of the old *Empresses*.

Minnesota and *Dakota* at Smith Cove wharf.

Developments of equal interest were taking place on the northern route, for James J. Hill and his Great Northern Steamship Company had proceeded with his grandiose plan for the construction of two big liners to run between Seattle and the Orient. The *Minnesota* and *Dakota* were monster vessels for their day, had a gross tonnage of 20,718 tons, and could each carry the fantastic total of 22,740 tons of cargo. Their weakness lay in their slow speed, and, in addition, they proved to be singularly unlucky ships. Nevertheless, for a time Hill made a formidable showing in the North Pacific. He arranged to have the big freighters *Shawmut* and *Tremont*, which were owned by the Boston Steamship Company, run opposite the *Minnesota* and *Dakota*. Three smaller vessels of the Boston Company's fleet maintained a second service in co-operation with three N.Y.K. liners. By 1906 Hill thus had ten steamers operating in connection with the Great Northern Railway, including the two largest ships on the Pacific, and might well feel that he was leaving all competitors far behind.

In spite of this the Canadian Pacific continued to rely upon the now aging *Empresses* to maintain its prestige in the trans-Pacific trade. Early in 1903 the Company had extended its shipping interests to the Atlantic by purchasing the fleet of the Beaver Line, and its neglect of the Pacific was undoubtedly largely due to its preoccupation with this new venture.

In 1906 a modest improvement was made in the Oriental service when the former Beaver Line steamer *Monteagle* was transferred from the Atlantic to the Pacific. She was a sturdy twin-screw vessel of 6,163 tons gross and was completed in 1899. She was one of a very successful series of freight and cattle boats, and had seen service as a transport during the South African War. Originally she was intended to carry only six cabin passengers. Before she left for the Pacific, however, she was refitted at Liverpool to carry 97 cabin class and as many as a thousand Orientals in the steerage. She then loaded a full cargo of Welsh coal for the Admiralty at Newport, and proceeded to Hong Kong by way of Teneriffe and Durban. She sailed from Hong Kong on her first trans-Pacific voyage on May 2, 1906, and arrived in Vancouver on the 26th. One of the newspapers remarked at the time that there was "nothing remarkable about the *Monteagle*."[49] In a sense this was true; yet in the course of a few years she acquired an excellent reputation. She was noted for her steadiness and, although her accommodation was far from elaborate, at least one of her captains remembers her as the only ship he ever commanded in which he never received a complaint from a passenger.

James J. Hill.

Minnesota.

Dakota.

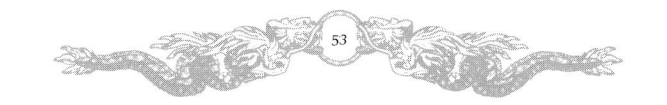

Captain A.H. Reed, later Harbour Master of Vancouver, on her bridge. Outside the Narrows she encountered fog, and presently collided with the coastal steamer *Charmer*. The *Tartar* was badly holed and was beached in English Bay, where she lay for some days. She was repaired in the old Esquimalt dry-dock, but various small misfortunes caused further delays, and it was not until December 15 that she finally reached Yokohama.

Monteagle ashore in the typhoon September, 1906.

Tartar beached near Siwash Rock off Stanley Park, Vancouver after her collision with *Charmer*.

The *Monteagle* was brought out by Captain H. Parry, of the trans-Atlantic fleet, who handed her over at Vancouver to Captain Samuel Robinson, formerly commander of the *Athenian*. Her Chief Engineer was J.B. Penty, who came ashore after a few voyages and took over the post of Engineer of the new Empress Hotel, then under construction in Victoria.

Disaster almost overtook the *Monteagle* after she had completed only two round trips across the Pacific, for she was caught in Hong Kong by the great typhoon of September 18, 1906. The *Empress of Japan*, which was also in port, rode out the storm successfully, but the *Monteagle* was driven ashore and damaged her stern-post. As a new one had to be forged in England, she was laid up all winter and did not resume service until March, 1907.

A few months later, early in August, it was announced that the *Athenian* and *Tartar* had been sold to Japanese purchasers. On the 22nd the *Athenian* sailed from Vancouver for the last time, under the command of Captain A.O. Cooper. Her final voyage was made without incident, but the career of the *Tartar* had a more exciting conclusion. She sailed from Vancouver on October 17, 1907, with

Neither the *Tartar* nor the *Athenian* was operated by their new owners for long, and both went to the ship-breakers in 1908.

Such traffic statistics as are available indicate that the old *Empresses* retained their popularity to a surprising degree throughout these exciting times. The reason is not far to seek. Though surpassed in size and speed, they still offered the fastest regular schedule across the Pacific, and the reliability of their service remained proverbial. These were considerations of great importance to the silk and tea trades, and it was because they could meet these specialized demands that the prosperity of the *Empresses* continued.

Their success in attracting first-class passengers is more difficult to explain. Their faster schedule accounts for it in part, and they benefited greatly from through bookings to and from the Canadian Pacific Railway. But there is no doubt that the yacht-like lines which had caught the imagination of the travelling public when they first entered service, together with the reputation they had established in the intervening years, were important factors. For, considered objectively and stripped of the glamour which surrounds their memory, the old *Empresses* cannot be said to have been specially attractive ships in some respects. They were speedy and safe, but wet and very uncomfortable in a rough sea. They could roll and pitch in an astonishing way, and upon occasion threw the clinometer beyond 45 degrees. They were fitted with bilge-keels in 1901, which reduced their rolling considerably, but there is no doubt that the *Monteagle* was the comfort ship of the old fleet.

Empress of India: the comfortably appointed cabin of the Master. Here it is the personal belongings of Captain O.P. Marshall that bring a touch of home to the otherwise rather cramped quarters.

It is interesting to recall some details of their passenger accommodation. Even by the standards of 1908 it was becoming antiquated. The largest of the three public rooms for first-class passengers was the dining saloon, which was at the forward end of the upper deck. The two long tables down the centre of the room, and the dozen smaller tables along the walls, could seat a total of 104 persons. The style of decoration used is well illustrated in the accompanying photograph. The saloon measured about 36 by 48 feet, and its dome occupied the centre of the library, or lounge, which was on the promenade-deck above. This was a smaller room, about 30 feet square, decorated in a similar style. The smoking-room, which occupied the traditional position farther aft, was smaller still. All the furniture in all three rooms was either built-in or screwed down, which was just as well, in view of the lively way the *Empresses* behaved at sea.

The first-class cabins were mostly outside rooms, and were well fitted for their day. Almost all of them had three berths. There was no such thing as a private bath on board, and the "special suites of staterooms" referred to proudly in the early handbooks were nothing more than four larger cabins on the promenade-deck, which boasted real bedsteads and sofa berths. About 160 first-class passengers could be carried, and cabins for another 40 persons were provided aft in what was sometimes called second class, and at other times intermediate. Accommodation in the steerage varied in extent, for as much 'tween-deck space as was required could be fitted up at short notice if an exceptionally large number of Orientals booked passage.

Two other important reasons for the success of the *Empresses* must not be overlooked. In the first place, they were kept in good condition. Upkeep was never stinted and they were thoroughly overhauled at Hong Kong each year. In the second place, they were well run, and had the good fortune to attract a large number of efficient and popular officers.

Of the three original commanders, Captain O.P. Marshall of the *Empress of India* was easily the favourite. He was popular with both crew and passengers, and took such care of his ship that she was referred to humorously by those in the service as "Marshall's private yacht." She was his last command, for he remained in her until May, 1905, when he resigned to become an Elder Brother of Trinity House. It is said that he received this appointment, for which he was admirably qualified, through the good offices of the Prince of Wales, later King George V, who, as Duke of York, had visited British Columbia in 1901. The Royal party travelled from Vancouver to Victoria in the *Empress of India* on October 1 and returned in her on the 3rd. The Duke was much impressed, both by the smartness with which the liner was handled and by the personality of her commander.

Aft end of the Grand or Dining Saloon of the *Empress of India*.

Queen Victoria, Empress of India.

Tz'u-hsi, Empress Dowager of China.

Shoken, Empress of Japan.

The three Empresses after whom the ships were named.

Athenian, oil. Collection: Vancouver Maritime Museum.

Monteagle, mixed media. Collection: Vancouver Maritime Museum.

Empress of China, mixed media. Collection: Vancouver Maritime Museum.

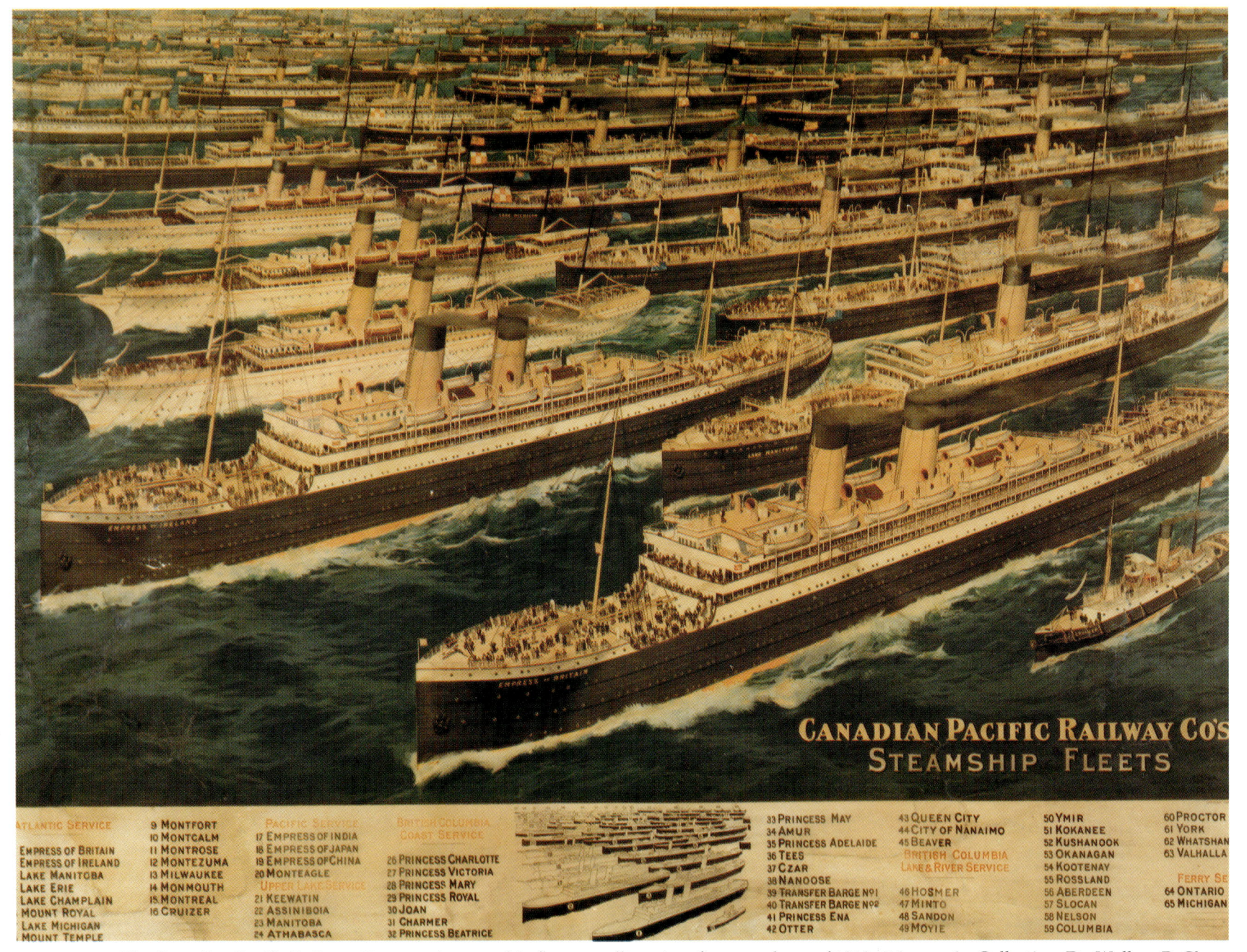

The Canadian Pacific Railway Company's steamship fleets, totalling sixty-five vessels, as of 1910, lithograph. Collection: Dr. Wallace B. Chung

Empress of Australia, hand-tinted photograph.
Collection: Vancouver Maritime Museum

Empress of Australia, Cruise brochure, 1937.
Collection: Vancouver Maritime Museum.

Empress of Australia, poster, Collection: Dr. Wallace B. Chung.

Empress of Japan (1): fire bucket.

Empress of Japan (1): bulkhead and rigging lanterns.

Empress of Japan (1): builder's model, c.1890/91. Collection: National Museum of Science and Technology and Canadian Pacific Limited.

Empress of Japan (1): chronometer by Joseph Sewill.

Empress of Japan (1): clock and barometer from Chief Engineer's quarters.

Empress of Japan (1), passing Brockton Point Light, Vancouver Harbour. Hand-tinted photograph.
All items shown on this and the preceding page are from the Vancouver Maritime Museum.

Empress of Asia, oil. Collection: Vancouver Maritime Museum.

1.) *India's* decorated Dining Saloon.
2.) Festooned C.P.R. Station in Vancouver.
3.) Duke & Duchess of York arriving Victoria, October 1901.
4.) *India* dressed for the Occasion.

The first Chief Engineer of the *Empress of India*, F.A. Wood, died at sea in 1892 and was succeeded by James Adamson, the Second Engineer. Adamson was as capable and careful an engineer as Marshall was a commander, and together they made a team which became famous in the *Empress* service. The *India* was undoubtedly the most economically run of the three pioneers, and her fuel consumption was consistently lower than that of her sisters. This result was obtained by good management and not by slower speed, and Adamson always regarded the records held by the *Empress of Japan* a little ruefully. He served as Chief in the *India* for twenty years and left her in 1912 to join the new *Empress of Russia*.

As noted previously, Captain Tillett, first commander of the *Empress of China*, left her in 1892 to become Marine Superintendent for the Canadian Pacific at Hong Kong. He was succeeded by Captain Rupert Archibald, formerly Chief Officer of the *Empress of India*. Although the *Empress of China* was the unlucky ship of the three, every one agreed that this was not the fault of her popular skipper. Captain Archibald commanded her for over nineteen years — the longest term any *Empress* captain ever served in a single ship. He seems to have looked back with some regret to the days of sail, for he made much more use of the canvas with which all the *Empresses* were originally equipped than did his brother officers.

Ill-health compelled Captain George A. Lee of the *Empress of Japan* to resign in August, 1900, and he spent the rest of his life in retirement in England. His successor was Captain Henry Pybus, one of the most prominent figures in the history of the old *Empresses*. Captain Pybus came to the Pacific as Chief Officer of the *Empress of China*, and in 1892 became Chief of the *India* and relieving captain for the fleet. Though somewhat of a martinet, Pybus was an able navigator, and when he was on the bridge things were likely to happen. Thus it was while he was relieving in the *Empress of India* that she had her adventure with the cruiser *Olympia*, in 1896, and he was in the *Empress of Japan* when she made her record run in 1897. His first permanent command was the *Tartar*, in 1898, and from her he was promoted to the *Empress of Japan* in 1900. He retired in January, 1911, and lived in Vancouver until his death in July, 1938.

The last of the original officers of the *Empresses* to receive a command was Edward Beetham, who came out as Fourth Officer in the *Empress of Japan*, in 1891. His promotion was rapid, and within a few years he was next in seniority to Captain Pybus. As a consequence he succeeded Pybus as commander of the *Tartar* when the latter moved on to the *Empress of Japan* in 1900, and in 1905 Captain Beetham himself took over the *Empress of India* upon the resignation of Captain Marshall. In 1913 he moved on to the new *Empress of Russia*, and in 1914 came ashore in Vancouver as Marine Superintendent.

Three other *Empress* captains who were very well known in later years received their first commands while the old liners still headed the trans-Pacific fleet. Captain Samuel Robinson joined the *Empress of Japan* as a junior officer in 1895, and became Chief Officer of the *Empress of China* in 1899. In February, 1903, he was appointed Captain of the *Athenian*, and it will be recalled that he took over the *Monteagle* when she came to the Pacific in 1906. Upon the retirement of Captain Pybus, in 1911, he moved to the *Empress of Japan*. He was in her only two years, as he was sent to the Clyde to join the new *Empress of Asia* in March, 1913.

The early careers of Captain A.W. Davison and Captain A.J. Hailey closely paralleled that of Captain Robinson, for they were taking successive steps up the same ladder. Captain Davison joined the *Empress of China* as a junior in 1895, and after serving as Chief Officer in the *India* was appointed to his first command, the *Tartar*, in 1905. He succeeded Captain Robinson in the *Monteagle*, and in 1913 was promoted to the *Empress of India*, which he left early in 1914 to take over the *Empress of Russia*. Captain Hailey entered the service as Fourth Officer of the *Empress of Japan* in 1900, and after a spell in the *Athenian* returned to the *Japan* as her Chief Officer in 1905. His first permanent command was the *Monteagle*, but both before and after this appointment he made voyages as relief captain in the *Empress of India*. In 1914 he became her regular skipper and remained in her as long as she was in the Canadian Pacific service. It is interesting to note that Captain Hailey grew up across Morecambe Bay, within sight of Barrow-in-Furness, and well remembered the days when the old *Empresses* were taking shape in the shipyard there.

Analysis of these biographical notes shows that the three pioneers had remarkably few captains, considering their length of service. Though they sailed the seas for the Canadian Pacific for a total of seventy-five years, they had no more than twelve regular commanders between them.

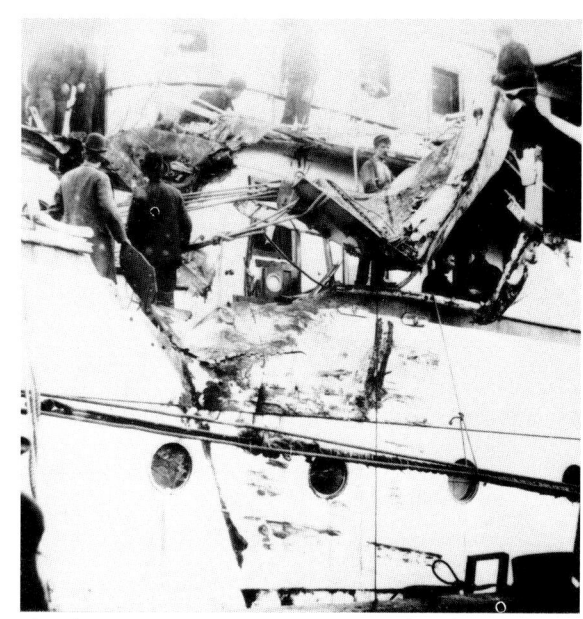

The damage to *Empress of Japan (1)* after her collision with barque *Abby Palmer*.

For purposes of record the following tabulation will be of interest:

COMMANDERS OF THE OLD "EMPRESSES"

Empress of India:
O.P. Marshall 1891-1905; Edward Beetham, 1905-13; A.W. Davison, 1913-14;
A.J. Hailey, 1914-15.

Empress of Japan:
George A. Lee, 1891-1900; Henry Pybus, 1900-11; Samuel Robinson, 1911-13;
W. Dixon Hopcraft, 1913-21; A.V.R. Lovegrove, 1921-22; A.J. Holland, 1922.

Empress of China:
A. Tillett, 1891-92; Rupert Archibald, 1892-1911.

A similar tabulation of the Chief Engineers of the old liners would not be of much greater length, and a few of the names which would appear should be mentioned here. The record of James Adamson, in the *Empress of India*, has already been noted. In the *Empress of Japan*, Thomas Tod was succeeded after a brief period by E.O. Murphy, who was Chief when she made her fastest passage in 1897. Murphy retired to go into business in Hong Kong in 1899, and his post was taken by William Auld, who was in the *Japan* for some fourteen years and was then promoted to the new *Empress of Asia*. James Fowler, first Chief Engineer of the *Empress of China*, resigned about 1900 to become a Lloyd's Surveyor. H.T. Richardson succeeded him, but after a time was appointed Superintendent Engineer for the Company at Vancouver. The next Chief of the *China* was James McGown, who served in her until 1902, when Richardson was promoted to the post of Superintendent at Hong Kong and McGown came ashore to take over his duties at Vancouver. James Neish then became Chief of the *China*, and in 1907 was succeeded by D.H. Mathieson, who served in the *Empress* until the end of her days.

Although small delays and misfortunes inevitably came their way, the *Empresses* suffered remarkably few serious accidents. One such occurred about 2:40 a.m. on the morning of November 6, 1900, when the steel barque *Abby Palmer* collided with the outward-bound *Empress of Japan*. The liner was struck on the port side, well forward, and suffered considerable damage. Fortunately this was all above the water-line. A lookout-man on the bow of the *Abby Palmer* jumped aboard the *Empress* as the vessels met, and it is amusing to note that he stayed with the ship and joined the crew. Captain Pybus contended that the lights of the *Abby Palmer* were improper, but the court of inquiry found the steamship to blame.

After the accident the *Empress* returned to Victoria for temporary repairs, and although she was nearly six days late in sailing, she managed to land her mails at Hong Kong within the contract time.[50]

Some three years later the *Empress of India* was involved in a much more serious collision. When darkness fell on August 17, 1903, she was steaming between Shanghai and Hong Kong. Shortly before midnight the officer on watch realized suddenly that she was coming up with another vessel, later found to be the small Chinese cruiser *Huang-Tai*, travelling on a parallel course. Exactly what happened in the next few minutes is still not entirely clear, but a press dispatch based upon Captain Marshall's report to his owners reads as follows:

> **When the Chinese gunboat was off the *Empress'* starboard bow, the captain of the cruiser suddenly starboarded his helm and turning to port attempted to cross the bows of the liner. The *Empress* immediately reversed her engines, trying to avoid being rammed broadsides by the cruiser. The liner sheered off sufficiently to catch a glancing blow from the bows of the cruiser instead of receiving the direct impact of the war vessel, which would probably have cut her in two. The cruiser struck the *Empress* near the starboard side of the bridge and in sliding off carried away some of the upper works of the liner. As she drifted back, the steamer was still working her engines to stop, and still steering to sheer off from the warship. The result was that the starboard propellor of the *Empress* smashed the side of the warship as the latter passed her stern.**[51]

Some of the commanders of the first three Empresses.

1.) Captain E. Beetham
2.) Captain A.J. Hailey
3.) Captain H. Pybus
4.) Captain S. Robinson
5.) Captain A.J. Holland
6.) Captain A. Tillett
7.) Captain O.P. Marshall
8.) Captain R. Archibald
9.) Captain A.V.R. Lovegrove

Robert Kerr: as coaling hulk, supplying *Empress of China* with fuel for her next trans-Pacific voyage.

It turned out later that the *Empress* had suffered relatively little damage, but the *Huang-Tai* was so badly holed that she sank. About 150 of her crew were rescued, but a group of officers refused to leave the ship and went down with her.

The sudden change of course made by the *Huang-Tai* has never been explained satisfactorily. Various stories have gone the rounds, one of which suggests that the collision was due to the mistaken interpretation of an order shouted to the helmsman on the bridge of the *Empress*, while another insists that the cruiser was making a deliberate attempt to sink the liner, because she was carrying Chinese political refugees.

A curious misfortune befell the *Empress of China* late in October, 1907, while she was tied up at the Canadian Pacific dock in Vancouver. About 6 p.m. a longshoreman on board made the startling discovery that the vessel was sinking. Firepumps were rushed to the dock, but lack of proper hose connections made them ineffective and by midnight the *Empress* was down by the stern and resting on the bottom. For a time she was in grave danger of rolling over into deeper water. Fortunately the coal hulk *Robert Kerr* was lashed alongside and held her upright. It was known that the trouble was due to an open condenser discharge, through which water had poured into the engine-room when the loading of cargo and coal brought it below the water-line, and a diver was hurried to the scene to close the offending valve. Early next morning the salvage steamer *Salvor* came alongside and her pumps had the *Empress* safely afloat in a few hours. Thanks to the heroic efforts of all concerned, she was able to sail from Vancouver on time, but dynamo trouble made it necessary to hold her overnight at Victoria.[52]

Fourteen months later, in February, 1909, the *Empress of China* was again in difficlty, this time in the Inland Sea of Japan. A shifting current carried her off her course and she ran ashore. Though she struck heavily, she was able to get off under her own steam three hours later. The damage suffered extended for a hundred feet of her length, but she was able to complete her voyage to Vancouver before going to Hong Kong for repairs.

In the autumn of 1906 the schedule of the *Empresses* was altered for the first time since 1891. Henceforth the vessels were expected to travel from Vancouver to Hong Kong in nineteen days, instead of twenty-one. This change was due to developments on the Atlantic, where the Canadian Pacific had recently placed in service the first *Empress of Britain* and the *Empress of Ireland*. These vessels were the largest and fastest in the Canadian trade. By speeding up the trans-Pacific liners, the Company hoped to be able to carry mails from Liverpool to Hong Kong in as little as twenty-nine days.

This was asking much of steamers which had been running for sixteen years, and the old *Empresses* were taxed to the limit by the new schedule. It left practically no margin for contingencies, and assumed that the mails would always reach Vancouver at least approximately on time. For a few months all went well, but early in 1907 the line incurred its first penalty for the late arrival of an *Empress* at Hong Kong. To add a touch of irony to the incident, it was the queen of the fleet, the *Empress of Japan*, which fell behind the contract time. The fault was not really hers, for the English mails were over four days late in arriving in Vancouver, and it was obviously impossible for her to complete the voyage to Hong Kong in only fourteen days.

It was evident that new tonnage was needed on the Pacific if the faster schedule were to be maintained satisfactorily. In January, 1907, D.E. Brown, an official of the Company, stated that two new *Empresses* would be built at once, but no order was actually placed.[53] In July it was announced, on the much better authority of Arthur Piers, General Manager of the Canadian Pacific steamships, that plans for one new Pacific *Empress* were in preparation.[54]

A month later, shareholders found the following paragraph in the report submitted at the annual meeting of the Company:

> **The subsidy that is now being paid to your Company for the carriage of the mails between Liverpool and Hong Kong will expire in April of next year, and it is not improbable that a faster and more frequent service will be made a condition of its continuance. In view of this fact your Directors recommend that they be authorized to arrange for the acquisition or construction of two steamships to meet the requirements of your Pacific trade, or to build two larger and faster boats for the Atlantic service and transfer the *Empress of Britain* and *Empress of Ireland* to the route between Vancouver and Hong Kong.**[55]

But matters do not seem to have worked out quite as anticipated. Though the new contract signed in October, 1908, covered the carriage of mails all the way from Liverpool to Hong Kong, the service required was slower than that the Canadian Pacific was already maintaining.[56] Moreover the amount of the subsidy was reduced from £60,000 to £45,000 per annum.

No doubt these circumstances account for the fact that nothing more was heard about the new *Empresses* for several years. Meanwhile the old steamers carried on with remarkable regularity and success. Competition ebbed and flowed in a curious way. On the San Francisco route the Toyo Kisen Kaisha placed in service two fine new turbine steamers, which were the fastest and most modern ships on the Pacific. On the northern route, James J. Hill's formidable merchant fleet dwindled rapidly. The *Dakota* was wrecked, the Boston Steamship Company's steamers were withdrawn, and only the ships of the Nippon Yusen Kaisha and the single American liner *Minnesota* remained. Through it all the *Empresses* continued to offer the shortest route to the Orient. Though they were equipped with wireless in 1909,[57] no great attempt was made to bring their passenger accommodation up to date. But if their deficiencies were apparent, so were their low capital and maintenance charges.

In the summer of 1911 it was announced at long last that two new *Empresses* had been ordered from the Fairfield Shipbuilding Company, builders of the *Empress of Britain* and *Empress of Ireland*. The assumption was that the new liners and two of the old steamers would maintain a fortnightly service to the Orient. This gave rise to some speculation as to the fate of the third old *Empress*, but this ended a few weeks later when the *Empress of China* was wrecked on the Japanese coast.

The unlucky ship of the fleet met this final misfortune of her career on July 27, 1911. She had just come safely through a typhoon, and was proceeding cautiously through a fog-bank, when she struck the Mera Reef, off the entrance to Tokyo Bay. The engines were put astern, but she was found to be hard aground. All the passengers and most of the crew were soon taken off by small craft which came out from shore. No one was injured. The official inquiry found that the accident was due to the fact that the *Empress* had been carried 18 miles off her course "by a strong and unusual current, of the existence of which the master had no knowledge and no means of knowing, and to the mistiness and obscurity which left him in ignorance of his proximity to the shore."[58]

The *Empress of China* was so firmly embedded on the reef that salvage operations proved difficult and costly. It was not until December 12 that she was floated and taken to Uraga for docking. Several months later it was decided to abandon her to the underwriters. They, in turn, disposed of her to shipbreakers. The price is said to have been $65,500.[59]

Captain Archibald stood by his ship until illness compelled him to leave her, shortly before she was floated. In March, 1913, he succeeded J.A. Fullerton, who had held the post since 1888, as ship's husband at Vancouver. He retired in 1914 and lived in North Vancouver until his death in May, 1936, at the age of 82.

The interval between the loss of the *Empress of China* and the completion of the new *Empresses* was a difficult one for the Canadian Pacific. The *Monteagle* had to be pressed into the mail service, for which she was too slow and inadquately fitted. It is significant that first-class bookings fell off 60 per cent in 1912 as compared with 1911. No wonder everyone in the service looked forward to 1913 and the arrival of the new steamers.

The story of the *Empress of Russia* and *Empress of Asia* lies outside the scope of this article, which is concerned with the older units of the fleet, but their chief characteristics may be stated briefly. Their length overall was 592 feet and their gross tonnage 16,900 tons. In 1913 they were exceeded in size on the Pacific only by Hill's lonely giant, the 20,718-ton *Minnesota*. Their construction aroused considerable interest, for they were the first large steamers to have cruiser sterns. This novelty in design, together with their three large funnels, gave them a distinctive appearance which was much admired, and which

Empress of China aground on Mera Reef at entrance to Tokyo Bay, July 27, 1911.

was copied in all later Pacific *Empresses*. Their turbine engines, driving quadruple screws, enabled both sisters to exceed 21 knots on trial. As their passenger accommodation was luxuriously furnished, it is not surprising that the two vessels cost the Company slightly over $5,000,000.[60]

The *Empress of Russia* was completed first and sailed from Liverpool in April, 1913, under the command of Captain Beetham. Her maiden voyage ended at Vancouver on June 7. On the last leg of her journey she travelled from Yokohama to William Head in the record time of 9 days 5 hours 29 minutes. Like the *Empress of India* before her, the *Russia* thus ended her first passage Queen of the Pacific. She was joined presently by the *Empress of Asia,* Captain Samuel Robinson, which arrived in Vancouver on August 31.

Experience was to prove that the *Empress of Russia* and *Empress of Asia* were indeed the fine, soundly-built vessels which they appeared to be. In particular, the years were to show that their builders had anticipated the subsequent trend of liner design to an astonishing extent. When new, in 1913, they immediately restored the old prestige of the *Empress* line, for they were beyond dispute the fastest and best-equipped steamers in the trans-Pacific trade.

The new liners inevitably overshadowed the old *Empress of India* and *Empress of Japan*. Though admired as much as ever by ship-lovers, to most people they seemed all at once to be small in size and antiquated in equipment. Nevertheless they were still sufficiently fast to run in conjunction with the *Empress of Russia* and *Empress of Asia*, and the four vessels enabled the Canadian Pacific to inaugurate a fortnightly

Empress of Russia and *Empress of Asia* at Kobe.

service to the Orient. It took the old liners all their time to make the trip from Vancouver to Hong Kong, but the superior speed of the newer *Empresses* left them with a few days in hand. In June, 1914, it was therefore possible to extend the run of the *Russia* and *Asia* to Manila. Only two calls had been made there, however, before the whole schedule was disrupted by the declaration of war.

The *Empress of India* sailed from Yokohama just before the outbreak, and arrived at Victoria on August 14. She had made the crossing to William Head in 11 days 18 hours, which was the fastest time made by an old *Empress* in some years.[61] When she left for the Orient on August 22 it was realized that perils and adventures probably lay ahead, but few can have suspected that the famous pioneer of the *Empress* line was leaving Vancouver and Victoria for the last time. Officially, the voyage was number 120, outward; actually, it was her 238th trans-Pacific crossing. Captain A.J. Hailey was in command.

When the *Empress of India* reached Hong Kong she was ordered to Bombay, there to await orders from the Admiralty. She proceeded thither via Singapore. No lights were shown after she passed through Malacca Strait, as the German cruiser *Emden* was still at large in the Indian Ocean. At Bombay the *Empress* was examined by the Director of the Indian Marine, who informed Captain Hailey that his ship would be fitted out as a hospital ship, under the patronage of certain Indian royalty. The work of conversion was started at once and took about two months to complete. Meanwhile, in December, it was announced in London that the *Empress* had been sold to the Maharajah of Gwalior, who proposed to equip and maintain her as a hospital ship, at his own expense, as a contribution to the effort of the Empire.[62] The price paid was £ 85,000.[63] In keeping with her new purpose, she was christened *Loyalty* at Bombay on January 9, 1915.

Shortly after this she was ordered to the Persian Gulf. Then, when two days out at sea she was directed to proceed to Karachi. From there she sailed for Southampton, where she picked up sick and wounded Indian troops. In March she was back at Bombay. All this time she had retained her Canadian Pacific officers and crew. Upon her return to Bombay, however, Captain Hailey handed her over to the Indian Marine, and the last link with her original owners was broken.[64]

Empress of Japan (1) as an Armed Merchant Cruiser standing off the battle-scarred wreck of the German cruiser *Emden*, Cocos Keeling Island, November, 1914.

Her subsequent career as a hospital ship was a busy one. Press reports state that by the end of the war she had made forty-one voyages and carried a total of 15,406 patients. These included British, Indian, Chinese, East African, West African and West Indian troops, and a number of German, Turkish and Arab prisoners.

After the Armistice the *Loyalty* served briefly as a troopship. Then in March, 1919, she was sold to the Scindia Steam Navigation Company, of Bombay, which proposed to operate her between Indian ports, the Mediterranean and Great Britain. She was refitted as a passenger ship, and a sketch furnished by the Company indicates that some minor changes were made in her superstructure. Her period of service proved to be brief, for she was laid up at Bombay in March, 1921, after making only a few voyages to Marseilles and London. For two years she lay at anchor, neglected and rusting. Finally she was sold for scrap to Messrs. Maneckchand, Jivray & Co., late in February, 1923.[65] The records of *Lloyd's Register of Shipping* show that the actual work of breaking her up commenced in June.

Very different were both the war record and the subsequent career of the old *Empress of Japan*. She had sailed from Vancouver on July 23, 1914, and was nearing Yokohama when war was declared. She hurried on to Hong Kong, where she was at once fitted out as an auxiliary cruiser. She was stripped of movable fittings, but her passenger accommodation was not otherwise interfered with. Her armament consisted of eight old 4.7-inch guns, platforms for which had been provided at the time she was built. Some difficulty was experienced in securing a crew, but in spite of this she was prepared for sea in remarkably short order. When commissioned she joined the squadron under Rear-Admiral Jerram which was protecting the Eastern and Australian trade routes. While on war service she had a naval commander, but her regular skipper, Captain W. Dixon Hopcraft, stayed with her as navigator.

Her first cruise took her to Singapore, and then to Batavia, Macassar and Sandakar. On October 8 she was back in Hong Kong. For ten days she had had the honour of serving as flagship of Admiral Jerram, while *H.M.S. Minotaur* was detached on special duty. In addition, she had convoyed several captured enemy ships to Singapore. Her chief concern was the cruiser *Emden*, then at the height of her career as a commerce raider. Later the *Empress* was to have the satisfaction of retaking the British steamer *Exford*, which the *Emden* had seized and placed in charge of a prize crew.

From Hong Kong the *Empress of Japan* proceeded to Colombo, where she remained about three weeks. Her next cruise took her to the Red Sea, where she assisted the *Empress of Asia* and *Empress of Russia* in bombarding Turkish batteries and capturing armed dhows. When her services were no longer needed there, she was ordered to Bombay, where she was drydocked, overhauled and finally released by the British Admiralty.

As Captain Hopcraft was ill at the time, the *Empress* was taken to Hong Kong by her Chief Officer, Captain A.J. Holland. There another two months were spent refitting her for her regular run across the Pacific. It is amusing to note that while she served as an auxiliary cruiser the *Empress* retained her white hull and yellow funnels. When turned back to her owners, however, she was painted grey as a precautionary measure. As events turned out, she never regained her familiar colouring, for the hulls of the *Empresses* were all painted black for some years after the Great War.[66]

The *Empress of Japan* sailed from Hong Kong on December 1, 1915, and arrived in Vancouver on the 21st. As the *Empress of Russia* and *Empress of Asia* also returned to their regular run in the spring of 1916, the Canadian Pacific service reverted for a time more or less to normal. Later, however, the two big ships were again commandeered, and only the *Empress of Japan* and *Monteagle* were left on the Pacific. Even so, many wartime duties came their way. The *Empress* carried thousands of Chinese labourers, who were either bound for France or returning home, and in 1919 she brought many of the British and Canadian troops in the Siberian Expeditionary Force back from Vladivostock.

When she finally returned to her normal trade it was clear that her remarkable career was nearing its end. True, she was still sound and trim, and lovely to look upon. But she was nearly 30 years old, and was obviously too small to be retained longer than necessary. In the Fairfield yard the new *Empress of Canada* was already taking shape, and presently it was announced that the German liner *Tirpitz* had been acquired and would come to the Pacific as the *Empress of Australia*.

The *Empress of Canada* was expected to be ready for service in 1921, but her completion was delayed, and the *Empress of Japan* was reprieved for another year. In the interval Captain Hopcraft, who had been her commander since 1913, was succeeded by Captain A.V.R. Lovegrove. He remained in her for only three voyages, after which she was taken to Hong Kong by her Chief Officer, Captain P. Sinclair, and there turned over to Captain A.J. Holland, in April, 1922.

On June 1 she sailed for the Orient on her 158th and final round trip. On her return she passed through the First Narrows and tied up at Vancouver for the last time, on July 18. The next day the proud new *Empress of Australia* arrived from England to take her place in the sailing schedule.

Few ships have served their owners as well, and caused them as little anxiety, as the old *Empress of Japan*. From first to last she was in commission for over thirty-one years. For twenty-two of them she held the Pacific record. She crossed the Pacific no less than 315 times, yet the collision with the *Abby Palmer*, in 1900, was the only serious accident in which she was ever involved. She steamed in all a total of

Figurehead of *Empress of Japan* (1) a few years after mounting on the foreshore of Stanley Park, circa 1929.

over 2,000,000 miles, 62,000 miles of which she covered while in the service of the Admiralty as an auxiliary cruiser.

During the longshore strike of 1923 the old *Empress* was used as a floating hotel for stevedores. Except for this interlude she swung at anchor in Vancouver Harbour for almost four years. Finally, in the spring of 1926, she was sold to Victor Lamken, who acted on behalf of R.A. Mahaffay, of the Railway Equipment Company, of Tacoma. It was said at the time that she would be dismantled and the empty hull sold as a barge. Actually, however, she was broken up by slow degrees in North Vancouver by R.J. Christian, a local contractor.

Two relics remain in Vancouver to recall the memory of the beautiful old liner. Her bell was purchased by F.H. Clendenning and presented to the Merchants Exchange. Her dragon figurehead was acquired by the Vancouver *Daily Province*, and was erected in Stanley Park, not far from the First Narrows, through which the *Empress* passed so many times.

In conclusion, a word should be said about the later years of the *Monteagle*. She was in Vancouver when war was declared and was held in port for a time as a precautionary measure. She finally got away to the Orient on August 19. In September she was taken over by the Admiralty at Hong Kong. She was released early in 1915, but was taken up again in 1918 and for a time in 1919. Most of her time was spent in the Pacific, though upon occasion she travelled as far afield as Suez. She carried many coolies from North China, and in 1919 called several times at Vladivostock to repatriate prisoners of war from Russia.

One of the few exciting incidents in the career of the *Monteagle* came in 1921, when she rescued the survivors of the French steamer *Hsin-Tien* under conditions of great difficulty. The gallantry of her crew was suitably recognized by the French Government.

Empress of Japan (1): bell presented to the Vancouver Merchants' (now Grain) Exchange by F.H. Clendenning. Collection: Vancouver Grain Exchange.

Upon the arrival of the new *Empress of Canada* and *Empress of Australia* in the summer of 1922, the *Monteagle* was withdrawn from service and laid up in Vancouver Harbour. In September it was decided to send her to the Atlantic. She loaded a full cargo of lumber and sailed for St. John, New Brunswick, on the last day of the month. There she lay idle for a second time, after which she crossed the Atlantic to London.

Her last days have been described by Frank C. Bowen. It seems that she was laid up in the East India Dock during most of 1923, and was then taken down the Thames to Southend, where she swung at anchor for another two years. She was retained all this time because the Canadian Pacific had intended to rebuild her as a modern cargo-carrier and rename her *Belton*. Owing to rising costs and low freight rates the plan was abandoned. In the spring of 1926 — about the same time her old running mate, the *Empress of Japan*, was sold — the *Monteagle* was disposed of to Messrs. Hughes Bolckow, of Middlesbrough. The purchase price was £10,750. Subsequently she was towed to Blyth, where many great liners have met their end, and broken up.[67]

So passed a famous generation of ships from the Pacific.

Empress of Japan (1): being dismantled at Vancouver and sold as scrap, 1928.

III.

EMPRESS ODYSSEY: A HISTORY OF THE CANADIAN PACIFIC SERVICE TO THE ORIENT, 1913-45[1]

1.

The harbours of Vancouver and Victoria are filled with ships, but for the ship-lover something is lacking from the scene. No white-clad *Empress* liners glide into port, or lie resplendent, tied up to their accustomed berth. World War II broke the rhythm of the famous service to the Orient that had been conducted without interruption, except for a few months in 1914-15, for a full half-century. The initial sailing of the line was made by the old *Empress of India* in April, 1891, and the *Empress of Asia* completed the last regularly scheduled voyage in January 1941. A few months later the new *Empress of Japan* made a secret wartime visit to Vancouver, but this was to be the last appearance of an *Empress* in the harbour she and her running mates had known so well.

By 1945 three of the four *Empresses* that had maintained the trans-Pacific service had been destroyed; only the *Empress of Japan*, renamed *Empress of Scotland*, survived. There seemed to be little hope that the line would rebuild its fleet and emerge as happily as it had done from an earlier crisis of a very different kind that had developed a few years before the First World War. The three original *Empresses* were then still on the run, and the Canadian Pacific's troubles arose from its tardiness in recognizing the fact that its wonderful old ships could not carry on indefinitely. Small as they were (their gross tonnage was only 5,940), they had nevertheless been the largest and fastest steamers on the Pacific when they were completed in 1891. Few ships have become so well known so quickly, but when twenty years had passed without any new *Empresses* being added to the fleet, the prestige of the service began at last to decline. Thanks to their reputation, their reliability, and the shorter northern route upon which they operated, the old liners still managed to hold their own as mail and silk carriers, but as passenger ships they had been definitely outclassed. Competition had been severe ever since the turn of the century, when the Pacific Mail Company acquired four new liners, all of them twice as big as the *Empresses*, for the run from San Francisco to the Orient. It had been still more severe since 1908, when the Pacific Mail's Japanese rival, the Toyo Kisen Kaisha, placed in service the *Chiyo Maru* and the *Tenyo Maru*. These turbine-driven sister ships were the fastest and best equipped liners yet built for the Pacific. Their length over all was 575 feet, and their gross tonnage 13,450. On trial they attained a speed of 20.6 knots, and on one of her first voyages the *Tenyo Maru* averaged 18.25 knots from Honolulu to San Francisco.[2] This was far beyond the capabilities of the old *Empresses* in their palmy days, let alone their old age. True, it soon became apparent that the Japanese did not intend to operate their new ships at more than about 15 knots, but they could always change their minds.

When the Canadian Pacific decided at last to take the measure of these rivals, its first plans were conceived on a grand scale. About the beginning of 1910 the Fairfield Shipbuilding and Engineering Company of Govan, on the Clyde, was asked to prepare preliminary designs for ships no less than 700 feet in length. An air of mystery surrounded the inquiry, for only a few high officials knew that it came from the Canadian Pacific. Within the yard it was referred to merely by the curious code word "UBAB." The proposed ships were much larger than any that the Fairfield Company had yet built, and the draughting-rooms buzzed with excitement. Unfortunately disappointment soon followed, for it became apparent that 700-foot vessels would cost much more than the Canadian Pacific cared to spend. In the course of a twelve month the design was completely revamped twice — once for a proposed length of 650 feet, and then for the overall length of about 600 feet that was finally accepted. This brought the hull dimensions down to figures that the yard had exceeded in some respects in the Cunarders *Campania* and *Lucania* as long before as 1892, but in gross tonnage the final design still established a record for Fairfield.[3]

The contract for the new liners was finally signed in the early summer of 1911, and the news was announced in Vancouver by W.T. Payne, then Oriental manager of the *Empress* service, as he was about to sail in the *Empress of China* for his headquarters in Yokohama.[4] It was assumed that the two new ships and two of the old *Empresses* would between them maintain fortnightly sailings across the Pacific. This gave rise to some local speculation as to what would become of the third old *Empress*, and as if to settle the matter, the *Empress of China*, with Mr. Payne on board, piled up on a reef outside Yokohama on July 27 and damaged herself so severely that she was never reconditioned. In September the press reported that one of the new steamers would be named *Empress Van Horne*,[5] and if this quaint suggestion had been adopted one can only assume that the sister ship would have been called the *Empress Mount Stephen*. Fortunately the idea, if it was ever seriously entertained, was quickly abandoned, and early in October it was stated officially that the vessels would be named *Empress of Russia* and *Empress of Asia*.[6]

No one was surprised that the order went to the Fairfield Company, for the Canadian Pacific was already an old customer of the yard. The *Assiniboia* and *Keewatin* for the Great Lakes, the *Princess Charlotte* and *Princess Adelaide* for the British Columbia coast fleet, and the *Empress of Britain* and *Empress of Ireland* for the trans-Atlantic service had all come from Fairfield since 1906. The surprise lay in the characteristics of the new ships themselves. One might have expected them to bear at least a family resemblance to the Atlantic *Empresses*, but in fact it was quite otherwise. The *Empress of Britain* and her sister were orthodox in the extreme. They had old-style elliptical sterns, reciprocating engines, and lounges and cabins that recalled late-Victorian interior decoration at its plush- and drapery-clad worst. The *Empress of Russia* and *Empress of Asia*, on the other hand, incorporated many new ideas and anticipated the general trend of passenger ship design for many years to come. For this three men were largely responsible: Dr. Percy Hillhouse, naval architect for the Fairfield Company; W.D. McLaren, later a resident of Vancouver, who was then in charge of turbine research and design at Fairfield; and Major Maitland Kersey, who watched over the planning and construction of the ships on behalf of the Canadian Pacific.

The over-all length of the vessels was 592 feet, their width 68.2 feet, and their moulded depth 46 feet. Owing to small variations in design the *Empress of Asia* was slightly the larger of the two. Her gross tonnage was 16,909, that of the *Empress of Russia* was 16,810. Similarly, the *Asia's* displacement was 25,400 tons, while that of the *Russia* was 25,200.[7] The visitor on board had no difficulty in telling one sister from the other, as different schemes of decoration were used in their lounges and smoking-rooms. Externally, however, even an *Empress* officer could detect only one distinguishing feature: the wheelhouse of the *Empress of Asia* had portholes, whereas that of the *Empress of Russia* had square windows.

The *Empresses* were not the largest ships on the Pacific, as they were at first intended to be, for the Great Northern Steamship Company's *Minnesota*, of 20,718 tons gross, was still in service when they were completed.[8] But they were the fastest, and by far the best equipped and most modern in design. Amongst other things, they were the first big liners to have cruiser sterns, a feature now virtually universal. Dr. Hillhouse was responsible both for this innovation[9] and for the attractive and distinctive appearance of the vessels. Their cruiser sterns, long unbroken deck-houses, and three funnels set the general pattern that was to be followed in later *Empresses* for twenty years. To the best of their designer's knowledge they were also the first "four-compartment" ships — that is, the first liners in which four watertight compartments could be flooded without sinking the ship.

A maximum speed of 20.5 knots and a service speed of 18 to 19 knots were specified, and Parsons turbines were chosen as the best means of developing the required power. The whole machinery layout therefore became the responsibility of W.D. McLaren. Ordinarily a ship of the size would probably have had three turbines (one high-pressure and two low-pressure) driving three propellors. Mr. McLaren decided to use four turbines driving four propellors instead. This enabled him not only to keep the individual turbines conveniently small, but also to introduce an intermediate-pressure turbine into the series. This in turn increased efficiency and cut down fuel consumption. No large liner afloat had such turbines at the time the *Empresses* were designed.

Major Kersey took a special interest in the passenger quarters, which accommodated 284 in the first-class, 100 in second class, and 808 in the Oriental steerage. Every first-class cabin was either an outside or a Bibby-style room, but it is interesting to note that to begin with only the eight special suites were fitted with running hot and cold water. A big ship's plumbing and wiring, the complexity of which adds prodigiously nowadays to the cost of a liner, were still relatively simple in 1911. The public rooms were designed at the height of the enthusiasm for "period" styles that swept the seven seas in the years immediately before and after the Great War. It is the fashion now to poke fun at such rooms, but the fact remains that they were usually a vast improvement upon those of an earlier day. Few pleasanter dining saloons have been put afloat than those in the *Empress of Russia* and *Empress of Asia*, and the smoking-room of the *Asia*, which was finished in carved wood in natural colour, was a fine example of successful ship decoration.[10]

The keel of the *Empress of Russia* was laid on November 7, 1911. By that time the Canadian Pacific's need for new tonnage in the Pacific was acute, for the loss of the *Empress of China* in July had disrupted schedules badly. In 1912 the number of first-class passengers carried to and from the Orient fell to the all-time low of 649.[11]

Empress of Russia: Smoking Room.

Empress of Asia: Smoking Room.

Empress of Russia: Dining Room.

Empress of Asia: Dining Room.

Fortunately the Fairfield Company was able to deliver the new ships in relatively quick time. The *Empress of Russia* was ready for launching by August of 1912, and on the 28th she was sent afloat by Mrs. Wyndham Beauclerk, daughter of Sir Thomas (later Baron) Shaughnessy, then president of the Canadian Pacific Railway. The keel of the *Empress of Asia* was laid on December 4, 1911, and she was launched on November 23, 1912, by Mrs. G.M. Bosworth, wife of the manager of the Canadian Pacific's OceanSteamships. The *Russia* was ready for her trials in March, 1913, and the *Asia* followed at the end of May. The former was thus completed in less than seventeen months, and the *Empress of Asia* in less than eighteen months.[12]

Between them the new sisters cost just over $5,000,000.[13] This was looked upon as a vast expenditure at the time, but their performance on trial indicated that the company was getting its money's worth. The contract requirements were a speed of 20.5 knots on the measured mile, and an average of 20 knots on a 600-mile sea trial. The turbines were expected to develop about 22,500 shaft horse-power. Those of the *Empress of Russia* actually developed a maximum of 26,285 s.h.p., and she attained a speed of 21.178 knots on the measured mile. The *Empress of Asia* did even better. Her fastest runs were made at 21.43 knots, and her turbines developed 27,280 s.h.p. This was probably the only time in their whole careers that their turbines were forced to the limit, and the 600-mile sea trials gave a much better idea of the maximum speeds that might be expected in regular service. The *Empress of Russia* averaged 21,030 s.h.p. and a speed of 20.14 knots; the *Empress of Asia* — once more doing just a little better than her sister — averaged 21,810 s.h.p. and 20.33 knots. Equally satisfactory was the fact that the intended ordinary service speed of 18 to 19 knots was reached when the turbines were developing considerably less than the designed power.[14]

There had been talk of equipping the *Empresses* to burn oil, but they were completed as coal-burners. This is surprising, for even in 1913 oil fuel was coming to the fore on the Pacific. The *Chiyo Maru* and *Tenyo Maru* could burn oil or coal at will, and so could the new Canadian-Australasian liner *Niagara*. As in all coal-burning ships, poor quality coal or inefficient firemen could slow the *Empresses* down, but through the years they established a fine record for consistent performance, and rarely fell far behind schedule.

The *Empress of Russia* dropped anchor at Greenock, after her trials, on March 24, 1913. That same day she was formally handed over to her owners, and her log commences with the notation: "Hoisted C.P.R. flag." Her first commander was Captain Edward Beetham, who had joined the old *Empress of Japan* when she was first commissioned, and in recent years had been in command of the *Empress of India*. A.J. Hosken was chief officer, and James Adamson, another old-timer who had been in the *Empress of India* since 1891, was chief engineer.

The *Empress's* maiden voyage commenced at Liverpool on April 1, when she sailed with a large party of round-the-world excursionists. Proceeding by way of the Mediterranean and the Suez Canal, she called at Gibraltar and Monaco, passed through the Straits of Messina, paused at Port Said, gave her passengers time to see some of the sights in Colombo, visited Singapore, and tied up at Hong Kong on May 9. Twelve days later she set off to make the round of the Oriental ports she was to know so well in years to come: Shanghai, Nagasaki, Kobe and Yokohama. This first visit to Nagasaki was memorable, for between 8 a.m. and 2 p.m. on May 25 the human chains of Japanese coal-handlers, for which the port was long famous, swarmed up her sides and poured no less than 3,200 tons of coal into her bunkers. This was an average of 533 tons per hour — a record that has never been equalled.[15]

On May 29 the *Empress* left Yokohama and set off across the Pacific. In spite of strong winds, rough following seas, and some dense fog, she made steady progress, and completed the passage to William Head in 9 days 5 hours and 29 minutes. This reduced by more than 28 hours the old eastbound record of 10 days 10 hours, held for many years by the *Empress of Japan*. The *Russia's* average speed — about 19 knots — was higher than any other vessel on any competing route had ever averaged, and when she tied up in Vancouver, she was indisputably Queen of the Pacific. Quite as satisfactory from the point of view of her owners was the fact that she brought no less than 1,066 passengers — 198 of them in first-class — and a cargo that totalled 3,854 tons measurement.[16]

The *Empress of Asia* was delivered to her owners on May 31 and sailed from Liverpool on June 14. In order to avoid the extreme heat that prevails in the Red Sea during the summer months, she travelled to Hong Kong by way of the Cape of Good Hope. She arrived off Victoria late on the night of August 30, docked there the next morning, and tied up in Vancouver later in the day. Captain Samuel Robinson, one of the best known of all the *Empress* skippers, was in command, L.D. Douglas was chief officer, and William Auld was chief engineer. All three had been promoted to the *Asia* from the famous old *Empress of Japan*.

Monteagle: coaling at Nagasaki.

For the next few months the *Empress of Russia* and *Empress of Asia*, running in conjunction with the *Empress of India* and *Empress of Japan*, shuttled back and forth across the Pacific without incident. Then, in the spring of 1914, there came a spate of record-breaking. On May 3 Captain Robinson brought the *Empress of Asia* to William Head after a record run of 9 days 2 hours and 44 minutes from Yokohama. The average speed maintained was 19.19 knots.[17] If she had not encountered heavy gales that persisted for two days, the *Asia* would have done better still, for her best day's run was made at an average of 20.4 knots. But her performance did not go unchallenged for long. On May 29 the *Empress of Russia*, now commanded by Captain A.W. Davison, regained her laurels by completing a voyage in only 8 days 18 hours and 31 minutes, at an average speed of 19.86 knots — a record that was to stand for nine years.[18]

A month later, on June 29, the *Russia* added another page to the story of the *Empresses* when she tied up in the harbour at Manila. Hitherto the Canadian Pacific liners had not gone beyond Hong Kong, but it was found that the superior speed of the new *Empresses* left them with a few days in hand at the end of their run. The service was therefore extended to the Philippines, and the initial sailing fell to the lot of the *Empress of Russia*. Four weeks later the *Empress of Asia* followed, but thereafter the schedule was completely disrupted by the outbreak of war between Great Britain and Germany.

Empress of Russia: in Kobe.

Empress of Russia: Vancouver, 1913.

2.

For the *Empresses* the Great War proved to be a drama consisting of three acts and an interlude. The first act opened in familiar waters, but was played for the most part in the Indian Ocean. The second act was staged in the Red Sea. The interlude consisted of a return to regular trading across the Pacific, while the closing act took place in the Atlantic.

The *Empress of Asia* was actually requisitioned on August 3, before hostilities commenced. She was lying at Hong Kong, and the naval base there had been a hive of activity for some days past. She was quickly stripped of superfluous fittings, armed with eight old 4.7-inch guns, and prepared for service as an auxiliary cruiser. Mustering a naval crew proved to be a difficult problem, and when she finally sailed, her complement consisted of a strange conglomeration that included most of her regular officers, engineers, and Chinese seamen; men of the Royal Naval Reserve; detachments from the French Yangtse River gunboats and the Royal Garrison Artillery; and some Pathan Sepoys. Her first naval captain was Commander C.C. Walcott, R.N. (Ret.), who was succeeded later by Commander P.H. Colomb, R.N. Captain Robinson stayed with his ship, serving in the capacity of navigating officer.

Her first cruise took her to the Yellow Sea, where she joined a squadron headed by the old battleship *Triumph* that was keeping a watch on the German naval base at Tsingtau. When the entry of Japan into the war made her presence there no longer necessary, the *Empress* was sent to the Philippines. A dozen or more German merchantmen had taken refuge in various harbours there, and it was highly important that they should be prevented from sailing and carrying supplies to the enemy cruisers known to be close by.

The blockading squadron off the Philippines included the *Empress of Japan*, which had also been commandeered, and she and the *Empress of Asia* were joined presently by the *Empress of Russia*. The *Russia* had sailed from Vancouver on August 6, on schedule, in spite of the outbreak of war. Two days out her wireless operator picked up signals that two German vessels — one apparently near by — were exchanging in code, and more German messages were heard the next morning. Otherwise the voyage was completed without incident, and the *Empress* arrived at Hong Kong on the 22nd. At midnight on the 23rd she was taken over by the naval authorities, who fitted her out as an auxiliary cruiser. Like the *Empress of Asia* she was armed with eight 4.7-inch guns, but this armament was less formidable than it sounds; the guns were of an ancient pattern, and their effective range was only about 10,000 yards. Commander Archibald Cochran, R.N., took command, and Captain Davison became navigating officer. The *Empress of Russia's* first cruise was to Singapore, and from there she was ordered first to Hong Kong and then to the Philippines. The only excitement encountered came one day when the North German Lloyd steamer *Mark* was sighted on the horizon. The *Empress of Russia* gave chase, but in spite of her efforts to cut the enemy off the *Mark* managed to take refuge in American waters.

About the middle of September the first exploits of the famous commerce-raiding cruiser *Emden* became known, and to emphasize her presence in the Indian Ocean the *Emden* boldly bombarded and fired some oil-tanks at Madras on the 22nd. At this time the *Empress of Asia* and the Russian cruiser *Askold* — an ancient five-funnelled craft of questionable combat value — were escorting three transports that were carrying garrison troops home to Europe from the Far East. When they got as far as Colombo, the *Empress* was sent off in company with the British cruiser *Hampshire* to patrol trade routes and try to run down the *Emden*. Within a fortnight — although this was not known till long afterwards — the *Asia* came within an ace of doing so. She first got definite track of the raider on October 15, when she called at Diego Garcia, in the Chagos Archipelago, far to the south of Colombo. The little port had no wireless station, and its people were astonished to learn that war had broken out. The officers of the *Empress*, in their turn, were equally astonished to hear that the *Emden* had spent two days there the previous week. Captain von Muller had told the

Empress of Asia at rendezvous with *HMS Hampshire* prior to searching for *Emden*.

curious islanders that joint German-French-British naval manoeuvres were being held in the Indian Ocean, and several pleasant social functions had marked the *Emden's* visit. The *Hampshire* and *Empress of Asia* returned at once to Colombo, to protect shipping thereabouts. Then, on the 20th, they sailed with orders to sweep the seas between Ceylon and the Maldive Islands. All night long they steamed in line ahead, but when daylight came on October 21 — Trafalgar Day — they prepared to spread out, so as to scan the widest possible area. Their general course was to the southwest, and about 6:30 a.m. the *Asia* swung round to the northwest, the intention being that she should maintain this course for an hour or so, and then swing back to the southwest and proceed on a course parallel to that of the *Hampshire*. At this same hour, as it happened, the *Emden*, which had decided to leave the now heavily patrolled Colombo region and seek victims in safer waters, was in the same vicinity, steaming to the southeast. About 8 a.m. she and the *Empress of Asia*, steaming on virtually parallel courses but in opposite directions, cannot have been more than 10 miles apart. But it was a case of so near and yet so far, for the *Empress* failed to sight her quarry.

In the closing days of the search for the *Emden*, both the *Empress of Asia* and *Empress of Russia* were based on Colombo. On November 9, when the welcome news came that the raider had at last been found in the Cocos Islands and engaged by the Australian cruiser *Sydney*, both the *Empresses* were ordered to proceed thither immediately. Four days later the *Empress of Russia* met the *Sydney* at sea and took on board 230 survivors of the *Emden*. Many of the men were wounded, and it was impossible to care for them properly in the cruiser. Meanwhile search parties from the *Empress of Asia* had combed the Cocos Islands in an unsuccessful effort to find a landing party that the *Emden* had left behind, and the *Asia* later joined in a search for the raider's attendant collier.[19]

Before the end of 1914 both *Empresses* had shifted their base to Aden; the second act of their war drama had commenced. Turkey had allied herself with Germany on November 1, and it was essential that the trade and transport route from Aden to the Mediterranean be kept open and secure. The duties involved were of the most varied description. Some of the Red Sea lighthouses had to be taken over from the Turks or defended from them. At Hodeida the British and French consuls had been bundled off inland to Sana when hostilities commenced, and when their release had been arranged for, after protracted negotiations carried on through the intermediary of the Spanish authorities, the *Empress of Russia* sent in a steam pinnace under a flag of truce to bring them off. Later it was decided to take possession of Kamaran, the island port where many pilgrims bound for Mecca passed through quarantine. This the *Russia* accomplished, thanks to the combined efforts of her own guns and some Indian territorials brought along for the occasion. At one time the Turks were in a position to threaten Aden itself, and the *Empress of Asia* and *Empress of Russia* defended the port until British reinforcements arrived from Suez. A little later the *Minto*, of the Royal Indian Marine, was struck and damaged at Lohaia, to the north of Kamaran. The *Empress of Russia* answered her call for assistance, bombarded the port, and set a spectacular blaze alight when she fired the Turkish oil supplies that were stored there. Salif, Port Sudan, and Shaiksaid were the scenes of further incidents in which one or other of the *Empresses* was engaged. For the most part, however, they served as patrol ships. Five German steamers had taken refuge in Italian waters at Massaua, and one of their chief concerns was to keep an eye on them, and to prevent the dhows that dodged from one shore to the other from smuggling their cargoes across to the Turks. Some of these dhows the *Empresses* sank; others they towed to Aden. As dhow-towing in the stifling heat of the Red Sea was tedious in the extreme, the officers of the *Empress of Russia* devised slings that would hold a dhow against the ship's side, clear of the water, and so permit the liner to proceed at speed. One dhow, unable to stand the strain, collapsed amidships — an accident that called for elaborate explanations in high places!

Emden battered by *HMAS Sydney* and ashore at Cocos Keeling Island.

Guns of *Empress of Russia* firing on Kamaran in the Red Sea.

Capture of an Arab war-dhow.

Troops, guns and supplies being landed at Kamaran from *Empress of Russia*.

In the course of time it became evident that the valuable *Empresses* were being wasted in the Red Sea; the routine duties they performed could be done just as well by much smaller and slower ships. In the fall of 1915 it was therefore decided to turn them back to their owners. The *Empress of Russia* concluded her active naval duties at Bombay on October 19, and the *Empress of Asia* followed on the 22nd. The latter had travelled a total of 64,024 miles during her commission. From Bombay the *Empresses* proceeded to Hong Kong, where they were overhauled, refitted, and restored to their pre-war condition. By the early spring they were ready for service. Just before the *Empress of Russia* sailed from Hong Kong, instructions were received from Montreal that the sisters were to exchange commanders, and it was therefore Captain Robinson who brought the *Empress of Russia* into Vancouver on April 8, and Captain Davison who was on the bridge of the *Empress of Asia* when she docked four weeks later.[20]

The interlude in the war drama of the *Empresses* lasted for two whole years. In spite of mounting shipping losses, it was not until 1918 that they were again taken off their regular run to the Orient. The service they maintained was in itself important; they carried thousands of Chinese coolies, bound for France, where they worked in labour battalions behind the battlefronts, and both the Canadian Pacific and the British Government were reluctant to abandon the whole of the trans-Pacific trade to the Japanese. It was the need for transports to move American troops to Europe that finally led to the second requisitioning of the *Empresses*. The *Empress of Asia* left Vancouver in May, 1918, travelled to New York by way of the Panama Canal, and made six voyages to Europe before the end of the year. Five of these were to Liverpool, and the sixth to Brest. The *Empress of Russia* followed in due course, and made the first of her four trans-Atlantic sailings as a troop ship on July 6. Complete figures are not available, but we know that on five trips the *Empresses* carried a total of 14,489 officers and men. As many as 3,222 were carried by the *Empress of Russia* at one time.[21] Most of the voyages were without incident, and Captain Davison reported later that the *Empress of Asia* never sighted a submarine nor, so far as he knew, was she ever attacked. Upon one occasion it was known that a submerged submarine was lurking under the convoy, but at the surface the fog was so dense that it could take no action, and eventually it made off. Needless to say, this was before the days of Asdic, wolf packs, or the acoustic torpedo![22]

Quarantine Station at William Head near Victoria with new arrivals from China just off *Monteagle*.

Empress of Asia with some of the thousands of Chinese labourers bound for working battalions behind the frontlines in France.

Empress of Asia docking at Victoria on January 24, 1919 with over one thousand troops returning home.

Once the war ended, the Canadian Pacific was able to secure the release of the ships in remarkably short order. The *Empress of Asia* was able to sail from Liverpool for Vancouver on January 2, 1919, less than two months after the signing of the armistice. Travelling by way of Panama, she made the passage in 23 days, and the 1,100 veterans she carried received a great welcome at Victoria on January 24 and in Vancouver the next morning. The *Empress* was reconditioned by the Wallace yard, at North Vancouver, and the work was completed so quickly that she was able to sail for the Orient on February 27. Meanwhile the *Empress of Russia* had returned to her station by way of the Suez Canal. Leaving Liverpool on January 10, she picked up several thousand Chinese at Havre on the 14th and landed them safely at Tsingtau before proceeding to Hong Kong for refitting. In less than a month she, too, was ready for service, and on March 31 she tied up in Vancouver.

Both ships had fared better than most of the big British liners had done during the war. They were on active war duty for only about two years in all, and at no time were they badly knocked about. When they returned to peace-time service, they were virtually as good as new. Indeed, the only visible mark the war left upon them was a new colour on their hulls. When they went to the Atlantic in 1918, they were both given coats of camouflage, and the *Empress of Russia* received one of the most elaborate dazzle-paint jobs of the war. At refit time it was decided not to restore the white hulls that had been a distinctive feature of the *Empress* liners since 1891, and they returned to the trans-Pacific run with an all-over coat of light grey.

3.

The only running-mates available for the *Empress of Asia* and *Empress of Russia* in 1919 were the old *Empress of Japan* and the *Monteagle*. The latter was primarily a freighter, and had neither the speed nor the passenger accommodation necessary to enable her to fit comfortably into the mail service. Such a mixture of ship-types, ages, and sizes made the fleet difficult to handle, and all that could be done was to arrange a regular schedule for the two big liners and let the others fill in with extra sailings as they were able. This was regarded as a temporary arrangement only, for a new *Empress* was ordered soon after the Armistice, and the intention was that a second new liner should follow shortly.

The first two years of peace saw an unprecedented rush of traffic across the Pacific. To cope with it, various modifications were made in the passenger accommodation of the larger *Empresses*. Hitherto they had carried only three classes: first, second, and Oriental steerage. In 1919 staterooms for ninety-two persons in a new third class were added. The next year it became necessary to extend the first-class accommodation. By appropriating all the original second-class cabins, which were roomy and comfortable, the number of berths was increased from 296 to 374. New second-class quarters were added presently, further aft. In spite of this the ships were frequently taxed to the limit — indeed, demands were so pressing that they were often booked far beyond their nominal capacity. Saloon lists totalling 450 were not unusual, and the peak seems to have been reached in May,

Empress of Asia, also in camouflage.

1920, when the *Empress of Russia* arrived with no less than 480 in the first class. To accommodate them, cots had been placed in staterooms, officers had given up their cabins, and the patience and ingenuity of the ship's staff had been tried to the utmost.

It will be recalled that in 1912 the Canadian Pacific had carried only 649 first-class passengers to and from the Orient. In the year ended June 30, 1914 — the first twelve month in which the *Empress of Asia* and *Empress of Russia* were in service — the total jumped to 2,514. But in the year ended June 30, 1921, no less than 9,761 first-class passengers sailed by the *Empress* route[23] — a volume of traffic that must have brought at least $3,000,000 into the coffers of the company. Second class, the new third class, and Oriental steerage all added to the total, and the number of passengers carried in all classes, which had been 14,575 in 1913-14, rose to no less than 35,555 in 1920-21.[24]

Cargo holds as well as cabins were well filled, and the freight department shared in the boom. Silk was the most important single item in *Empress* inward manifests, and many immensely valuable shipments were landed at Vancouver. For example, in August, 1919, the *Empress of Asia* arrived with 10,800 bales of raw silk which, according to *Harbour and Shipping*, were valued at $8,500,000, and in addition she brought 2,053 cases of silk goods that increased the total to more than $10,000,000.[25] Tea, rice, and miscellaneous Oriental goods were for years the chief additional items in the cargoes carried from the Orient. Outward bound, the two staple items soon came to be spelter (zinc) and wheat products. When flour and wheat shipments first commenced on any scale, it was assumed that the trade

Empress of Russia in dazzle paint camouflage.

would be temporary, but between the wars a shipment totalling several hundred tons, and upon occasion consisting of as much as 2,300 tons, became a fixture in the *Empress* cargoes. On a smaller scale the same was true of spelter. Machinery, manufactured goods, timber products, and canned goods made up the bulk of the rest of the cargo.

In spite of their size the *Empresses* were not big cargo carriers; their dead-weight cargo capacity was only about 3,500 tons. They were primarily passenger and express ships, intended to carry shipments that were of great value, or for which rapid transit was essential. In order to share in the prosperous general freight business, the Canadian Pacific decided to bring to the Pacific two of the freight steamers that had been purchased during the war to run on the Atlantic. The first of these was the *Methven*, a 10-knot steamer of 4,852 tons gross, completed in 1906. She came to Vancouver by way of the Panama Canal, arriving early in March, 1919. More than a year passed before she was joined by the *Mattawa*, which came to the Pacific by way of Suez, and arrived in Vancouver for the first time in August, 1920. The gross tonnage of the *Mattawa* was 4,874, her speed was 9 1/2 knots, and she had been built in 1912. On some of their trans-Pacific trips these freighters turned back at Hong Kong, but the intention was that they should continue on and maintain a service as far as Singapore. As it turned out, their careers on the Pacific proved to be brief. By the end of 1920 the freight market was collapsing, and in January, 1921, both ships were laid up in Hong Kong. Later they were employed for a time in the Asiatic coastal trade. The *Methven* carried rice from Saigon, and upon one occasion went as far afield as the Persian Gulf, but before the end of 1922 both vessels had found their way back to the Atlantic.[26]

The *Methven* was the first permanent command of Captain L.D. Douglas, a future commodore of the Pacific *Empress* fleet, and such well-known figures as Captain A.J. Holland, Captain Herbert James, Captain A.V.R. Lovegrove, and Captain George Goold served in her or in the *Mattawa*.

The spring of 1921 was an interesting time for the *Empresses*. For one thing, each of them, as they came back into service after the usual annual overhaul, appeared in a new colour scheme. The light grey of 1919 now gave way to black hulls and white upper works; their funnels were buff, as before. For another, a new passenger service was started from Seattle to the Orient, and this inevitably aroused the spirit of competition. The five new American liners placed on the run were all of the well-known "535" type — redesigned army transports with a length of 535 feet, a gross tonnage of over 14,000, and a maximum speed of about 18 knots. Outwardly they were unattractive, and the arrangement of their cargo holds made it impossible to give them the spacious public rooms that characterized the *Empresses*. To compensate for this, special attention was lavished on their cabins, which were unusually large and abounded in private bathrooms. Nor were the Americans content to let the speed laurels of the *Empresses* go unchallenged, at least on paper. Time after time the claim was advanced — usually by the Seattle *Post-Intelligencer* — that silk brought to Seattle by the new steamers had been delivered in New York in less time than shipments landed in Vancouver by the *Empresses*. It was a difficult point to counter conclusively, but an opportunity came finally at the end of April, 1922. The American steamer *Bay State* (soon after renamed *President Madison*) left Yokohama for Seattle some time before the *Empress of Russia* sailed for Vancouver. Setting out in pursuit, the *Russia* overhauled the *Bay State*, passed her at sea, and arrived at William Head on May 7, after a passage of 8 days 21 hours and 43 minutes. The average speed maintained was 19.6 knots, which was only a quarter of a knot below the record established by the *Russia* in 1914. The *Bay State* took 10 days 5 hours and 22 minutes to make the crossing, and did not arrive until May 8. True, her captain contended that he was under orders not to exceed 17.5 knots, but this speed was below the voyage average regularly scheduled for the *Empresses*, and it was difficult to reconcile the captain's instructions with a claim that the line offered the fastest route for the shipment of silk from the Orient to New York.[27] Actually the *President Grant* (ex-*Pine Tree State*) seems to have been the fastest of the American liners, and she has to her credit a crossing at an average of 18.63 knots.

It may be well to add that this was not the only time that the *Empress of Russia's* record was closely approached. In the summer of 1919 the *Empress of Asia* completed a passage in 8 days 21 hours and 4 minutes at an average speed of 19.6 knots,[28] and in April, 1921, she came within minutes of repeating this performance.[29] Two months later the *Empress of Russia* crossed in 8 days and 21 hours at an average speed of 19.65 knots.[30] Later still, as we shall see, the *Empress of Asia* was to average more than 20 knots, and set a mark that neither of the sisters ever improved upon.

President Madison ex *Bay State*.

President Grant ex *Pine Tree State*.

A memorable adventure befell those on board the *Empress of Asia* in October, 1921. The *Empress* had sailed from Vancouver (as the superstitious will note) on the 13th. A week later she encountered what may well have been the worst storm to strike the Pacific in a quarter of a century. At noon on October 20 the barometer stood at 29.81. By 4 p.m. it had fallen to 29.29, and was still falling rapidly. At 10 p.m. the reading was 28.13. Even in the worst storms off the China coast the barometer rarely falls as low as 28.00, but on this occasion it fell much farther. At midnight it stood at 27.53, and at 1 a.m. reached the lowest level of all, about 27.48. By that time the needle was off the barograph, and only an estimate of its position was possible. It was the lowest point that Captain L.D. Douglas, who was in command, had ever seen the barometer reach in the course of a lifetime at sea. Fortunately the *Empress* was a little to the north of the centre of the storm, the velocity of which far exceeded 100 miles per hour. In spite of the pounding she received she suffered no structural damage, though at times her speed had to be reduced to as little as 8 knots. One of Captain Douglas's most vivid memories relates to a minor incident — the way in which the storm suddenly tore the canvas covers from the lifeboats. In his own amusing phrase, "they went away like a flock of gulls!"[31]

Captain L.D. Douglas.

4.

By the autumn of 1921 the new *Empress of Canada* was in the final stages of completion at Govan. Built by the same Fairfield yard that had constructed the *Empress of Russia* and *Empress of Asia*, she resembled them closely in general appearance. Internally, however, she was a very different ship, for her larger dimensions enabled her designers to plan her accommodation upon a more lavish scale. She had an extra deck, and the whole of her promenade deck was devoted to an elaborate suite of first-class public rooms. The older *Empresses* had boasted lounges, writing-rooms, smoking-rooms, gymnasiums, and veranda cafes. In addition to these, the *Canada* offered a long gallery, drawing-room, card-room, and children's room. She was also the first Pacific *Empress* to have such luxury-liner attractions as an elevator and a swimming pool. All her cabins had hot and cold running water, and forty of them had private baths or toilets.

Compared with the earlier *Empresses*, overall length had been increased from 592 feet to 653 feet, width from 68.2 to 77.5 feet, and gross tonnage from just under 17,000 to 21,517. The *Canada's* maximum displacement was 32,250 tons, and she was both the largest ship ever built for the trans-Pacific trade and the largest yet built by the Fairfield Company. Like most of the big liners built just after the Great War, the *Empress* was propelled by double-reduction geared turbines driving twin screws. She burned oil fuel, and her boilers were grouped compactly in two boiler-rooms under the two forward funnels. The third funnel was a dummy, added for the sake of appearance, and used only as a ventilating-shaft for the engine room.

The *Empress of Canada* had been laid down as soon as possible after the Armistice — too soon, as it proved, for her own good. Skilled labour and first-quality materials were both extremely scarce at the time, and her builders frequently found the going most difficult. Fine ship as she undoubtedly was, the *Canada* was never particularly lucky, and the minor mechanical troubles that dogged her throughout her career doubtless sprang in great part from the circumstances of her construction. Those circumstances, and the rapid rise in ship-building costs, had between them the further result of robbing her of a sister ship. A fourth big liner was required to maintain a fortnightly service across the Pacific, and by the summer of 1919 the *Empress of Canada's* projected sister was being referred to in the press by name as the *Empress of Australia*,[32] but within a few months plans for her construction were definitely abandoned.

Empress of Canada: in drydock, Victoria.

The *Empress of Canada* herself was launched on August 17, 1920, by Mrs. G.M. Bosworth, who, it will be recalled, had sponsored the *Empress of Asia* eight years before. The intention was that the *Canada* should leave Liverpool in March, 1921, and cruise to Vancouver by way of the Mediterranean, but the work of fitting her out progressed so slowly that this plan was soon abandoned. By June, 1921, the installation of her machinery had been completed, and she was able to leave the shipyard and run a series of builders' trials in the Firth of Clyde.[33] Newspaper stories credited her with having worked up to a speed of 25.6 knots,[34] but she was, in fact, quite incapable of any such performance. Moreover, the type of gearing used in the *Canada* required extremely careful handling when new, and it goes without saying that she was not forced in any way on this initial cruise.

Owing to a joiners' strike that kept work on her cabins and lounges at a standstill for many months, the *Empress* was not finally completed until April, 1922. Her official trials followed, but these were inevitably an anticlimax, thanks to the wild rumours that had circulated the year before. The maximum speed reached on the measured mile was 20.3 knots, with the engines developing 24,000 shaft horse-power. It will be noted that neither in power nor speed did she equal the showing made by the *Empress of Russia* and *Empress of Asia* in 1913. It was nevertheless clear that she would have no difficulty in maintaining the service speed of 18 knots that her owners had in mind, and on a 365-mile sea trial she averaged 20 knots, as required in the contract.[35]

Tripitz, later *Empress of Australia*, in drydock in her home shipyard at Stettin.

This sea trial ended at Falmouth, and from there the *Empress* proceeded to Hong Kong without delay, travelling by way of the Mediterranean. Captain A.J. Hailey was in command. In the Red Sea the new liner met the freighter *Methven*, which was returning to the Atlantic after her brief sojourn on the Pacific; otherwise the voyage was uneventful. On her first passage from Yokohama to William Head the *Empress of Canada* covered the distance in 9 days 2 hours — a good average run, but well below the marks set by the *Russia* and *Asia*. Victoria and Vancouver were both agog to welcome the largest ship ever to cross the Pacific, but one of those minor misfortunes that were to trouble the *Empress of Canada* so frequently marred the occasion. A case of smallpox developed on board, and this not only delayed her arrival until June 24, but made it necessary to cancel all festivities, including a reception to which thousands of invitations had been issued.

Less than a month later Vancouver welcomed another new *Empress*, and we must next describe the circumstances that brought this interesting vessel to the Pacific.

When shipbuilding costs soared in 1920-21, one of the factors that caused the Canadian Pacific to abandon plans to build a sister ship to the *Empress of Canada* was undoubtedly the fact that a number of German passenger liners, seized by the Allies at the end of the Great War, were coming on the market at knockdown prices. The *Canada* was costing £1,700,000; German ships of comparable size were selling for a fraction of this sum. To buy instead of to build would save time as well as money, and the company ended by making several purchases. One of these was the former North German Lloyd liner *Prinz Freidrich Wilhelm*, a vessel of 17,082 tons that had been operated for half a dozen years on the New York run. She was renamed *Empress of China*, and the work of refitting her, to make her suitable for the trans-Pacific trade, actually began. Before it had proceeded far, however, it was decided to bring a larger and much newer steamer to the Pacific in her stead.[36] This was the *Tirpitz*, one of a class of three ships that the Hamburg Amerika Line was building in 1914 for a new de luxe service to South America.[37] Her length overall was 615 feet, her width 75.2 feet, and her gross tonnage 21,861. She was thus much the same size as the *Empress of Canada*, and, like her, she had three funnels. But there all similarity ended. The *Tirpitz* had the old-style elliptical stern and the ungraceful, bulky upper works that were typical of the German ships of the period. Built in the famous Vulcan yard at Stettin, she had been launched on December 20, 1913.

In several respects she was an unusual vessel. To begin with, she had achieved a certain notoriety because rumour insisted that when the war was going well for the Germans, she had been selected to carry the Kaiser on the triumphal cruise that would have followed a German victory. It was even stated that her luxurious suites had been specially designed with this cruise in mind. The whole story is highly improbable, though work on her, which had come to a standstill, does seem to have been resumed for a time during the war, and her accommodation certainly included several palatial suites in which even an emperor should have felt at home. Her fittings throughout were elaborate, and her deck plans followed, on a reduced scale, those of the monster liners of the *Vaterland* class that the Hamburg Amerika Line was building at this same time. In particular, the uptakes to the two forward funnels were brought up through the passenger accommodation in two sections, some distance apart, and these did not come together until they reached the boat deck, at the base of the funnels proper. This made it possible to provide a broad hallway along the centre line of the ship, extending from one public room to another. On the promenade deck the effect was impressive, but on the cabin decks it gave rise to such a maze of corridors that the plan was seldom repeated.

Mechanically the *Tirpitz* was frankly an experiment. Her two sisters were fitted with machinery of orthodox design, but she had been chosen for a full-scale test of the hydraulic transformers upon which Dr. Fottinger had been working for some years. Instead of using mechanical gearing (as in the *Empress of Canada*) to reduce the high speed of her Brown-Curtis turbines to the relatively low speeds at which propellors operate most efficiently, the *Tirpitz* was fitted with what would nowadays be called a variety of fluid drive. In effect, her turbines drove water-pumps, and the water from these in turn drove water-wheels which were attached to the propellor shafts. It was an ingenious idea, and tests made with a full-scale set of turbines and transformers in 1912 seemed to show that it would prove reliable and economical in operation.[38]

The *Tirpitz* was completed about May, 1919, and after a period of uncertainty she was finally allocated to Great Britain, on reparations account. On February 3, 1921, she arrived at Immingham, and there she lay at anchor until she was purchased by the Canadian Pacific in July.[39] She was sent first to Hamburg, where she was dry-docked, refitted, and equipped to burn oil fuel instead of coal. Captain Samual Robinson arrived to take command of her early in 1922, and he

Empress of Australia,: Vancouver, July 21, 1923.

presently took her to the Clyde for a few last minute touches.[40] She had by this time been twice renamed. She first became the *Empress of China* (the other ship so named having by this time become the *Empress of India*), but this was soon changed to *Empress of Australia*. On June 16 she finally cleared for Vancouver, by way of Panama, and she reached her destination on July 19. Only a skeleton crew travelled out in her, but her complement was brought up to full strength as soon as she arrived in Vancouver. Many of those who joined her came from the old *Empress of Japan,* which had just completed her last voyage from the Orient. The *Australia* was given a thorough spring cleaning, took on cargo, provisions, and passengers, and sailed for Yokohama on July 28.

Her departure was a landmark in the history of the *Empress* service, for the Canadian Pacific now possessed the four big ships that were required to provide fortnightly sailings to the Orient. As all four of them were larger, and all but the *Empress of Australia* were faster than the ships of any other line, the competitive position of the *Empresses* seemed to be an exceptionally strong one. But unsuspected difficulties lay ahead, and another eight years were to pass before the state of the *Empress* fleet became really satisfactory.

Empress of Russia, oil. Collection: Captain S. Thrussell.

Empress of Asia: from Liverpool to Vancouver via the Cape of Good Hope. Promotional poster for the round-the-world cruise of the new *Empress of Asia*, June to August, 1913, Poster, Collection: Dr. Wallace B. Chung.

The art of poster design and colour has rarely been excelled
by the products of the 1920's and 30's. Here are two examples
of promotional posters commissioned by the C.P.R. in the mid-1920's
promoting its links and services to the Orient.

Empress of Canada, hand-tinted photograph. Collection: Vancouver Maritime Museum.

Empress of Japan (II), hand-tinted photograph. Collection: Vancouver Maritime Museum.

Table setting for two using Empress china and silverware. Collection: Dr. Wallace B. Chung.

Niagara, hand-tinted photograph. Collection: Vancouver Maritime Museum.

Empress of France, hand-tinted photograph. Collection: Vancouver Maritime Museum.

Souvenirs of the Trans-Pacific voyages in both the White Empresses and the ships of the Canadian-Australian Line. Obtained on ship and on shore by both passengers and crew.

Collections: Vancouver Maritime Museum, Dr. Ray Parkinson, Mr. Colin Maclock, and Captain G. McKee.

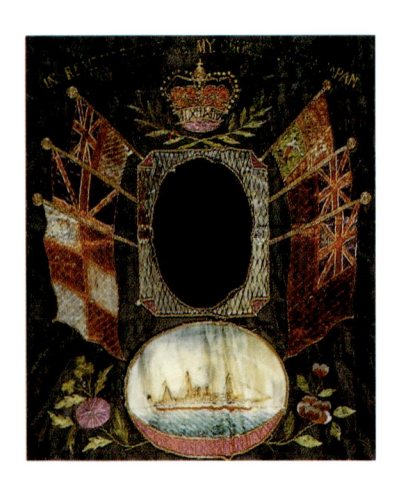

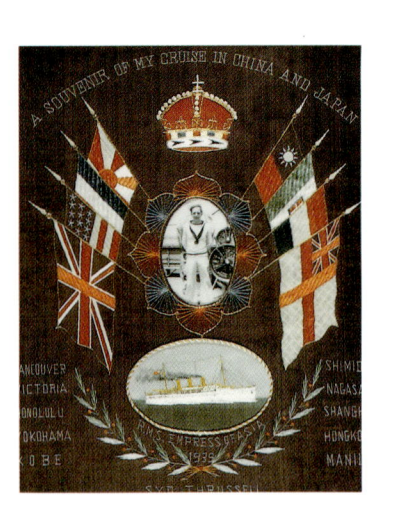

5.

The most serious of these difficulties was presented by the latest addition to the fleet, the *Empress of Australia,* whose engineers quickly discovered that they had a problem on their hands. She was fitted with water-tube boilers, and these were found to be poorly constructed and very hard on fuel. Equally important, the ship failed to develop her designed power and speed, and on her first trip to the Orient she lagged far behind the schedule maintained by the other *Empresses.* Her second sailing was delayed a week, in order that various adjustments might be made in Vancouver, and a 24-hour test run in Georgia Strait seemed to indicate that all was well. On September 28 the *Empress* therefore put to sea, bound for Yokohama. Two days later, however, a terrific thumping and crashing suddenly arose in the engine-room. The thrust blocks on one of the turbine shafts had failed, damaging the shaft itself, and completely disabling the turbine. Turning about, the *Empress* came slowly back to port, escorted part way by a salvage ship. Repairs were made in the Puget Sound Navy Yard, at Bremerton, where drydocks, heavy cranes, and other equipment were available. The work was carried out by the Todd Company, and the opportunity was seized to install improved oil-burners, which reduced somewhat the ship's excessive fuel consumption.

The *Empress* missed only one voyage to the Orient, and was back in service by the end of November. No further major machinery troubles developed, but it was no secret along the waterfront that she was still far from being a satisfactory ship.

A year after this mishap, sudden fame came to the *Empress of Australia* and to her commander, Captain Robinson. A minute or two before noon on September 1, 1923, when the *Empress* was lying at her wharf in Yokohama, on the very point of casting off and sailing for Vancouver, the first shock of the great earthquake that levelled most of Yokohama and Tokyo swept over the land. The ship shook and rocked so violently that Captain Robinson expected her masts and funnels to fall; a large slice of the wharf alongside subsided suddenly into the water, and from the vantage point of the bridge it was actually possible to see the land "rolling in waves apparently 6 to 8 feet high like a succession of fast moving ocean swells..."[41]

Empress of Australia in the earthquake-struck Port of Yokohama.

Bringing refugees to the *Empress of Australia* in her lifeboats.

The ruined city of Yokohama.

Empress of Australia: Dining Room.

Empress of Australia : Smoking Room.

Empress of Australia: Pool.

Empress of Australia: Lounge.

Empress of Australia: Sitting Room en suite.

Empress of Australia: Suite.

Empress of Australia: Bedroom Suite.

Empress of Australia: Drawing Room.

For a complete account of what followed, the reader is referred to the graphic report submitted by Captain Robinson to his owners, and subsequently printed in pamphlet form;[42] only a summary may be given here. For many hours the *Empress*, though serving as a haven of comparative safety to the refugees who crowded on board, was herself in extreme peril. Other ships in the harbour blundered into her, and her port propellor fouled a cable and held her prisoner close to the ruins of the wharf, which were soon a mass of flames. Huge masses of burning oil adrift in the harbour soon added to the dangers that beset her. But through it all her captain and crew worked calmly and ceaselessly to safeguard their ship, and to do their utmost to save life and lessen suffering. By slow degrees the *Empress* was edged away from her berth, but it was 36 hours before she was able to reach a safe anchorage. Later she moved outside the breakwater, and there her propellor was freed of obstructions by a diver secured from a Japanese man-of-war. With his ship once more functioning properly, Captain Robinson steamed back into the harbour, in order to do all he could to assist relief work. It was not until a week after the earthquake, by which time British and American warships had arrived with emergency supplies, that the *Empress* finally withdrew and sailed for Kobe with refugees.

Both the Canadian Pacific and Captain Robinson received and deserved many expressions of appreciation for the outstanding service the *Empress* rendered, and the following March a tablet was presented to the ship by the passengers who had been aboard her when the earthquake occurred.

Months before the Yokohama disaster it had been announced that the *Empress of Canada* would make a world cruise in 1924. Officially this was to start from New York on January 30, but so far as the ship herself was concerned, it commenced on January 4, when she sailed from Vancouver for New York, via Panama. The company was not above recognizing the publicity value of the fame Captain Robinson had achieved, and he was transferred to the *Empress of Canada* before she sailed. Captain Hailey took his place on the bridge of the *Empress of Australia*.

The *Canada's* cruise lasted four months. After a call at Madeira she visited various Mediterranean ports, sailed on to India and Ceylon, and proceeded thence to the Straits Settlements, the Dutch East Indies, the Philippines, China and Japan. Returning across the Pacific she deviated from her usual course in order to call at Honolulu and Hilo, and arrived back in Vancouver on May 24.

For the next two years the *Empress of Canada*, *Empress of Australia*, *Empress of Russia*, and *Empress of Asia* were all on the regular run to the Orient. It was known, however, that company officials were still far from happy about the *Empress of Australia*. Passengers found her luxurious lounges and well-fitted cabins pleasing, but down in the engine-room it was another story. There engineers fought a continuous battle to keep her on schedule, for she never developed anything approaching the speed of her running-mates. Thanks to great efforts below decks and a stretch of good weather, Captain Hailey was able to bring her to William Head on May 3, 1925, with a passage of 10 days 17 hours and 32 minutes to her credit, her average speed having been 16.4 knots, but this was her peak performance on the Pacific. She still burned a prodigious amount of oil, and, in addition, she was burdened with 1,500 tons of permanent ballast that the Germans had found it necessary to add, because her bulky upper works tended to make her top heavy.

About this time the Canadian Pacific reviewed the whole field of its ocean steamship operations, and several major decisions presently emerged. The first of these cleared the way for the great building program that was carried through during the next five or six years. Another concerned important units of the existing fleet. The company came to the conclusion that, from a long-term point of view, a thorough overhauling would prove to be a good investment. Early in 1926 it was announced in the annual report that a re-engining program would get under way immediately, and that the *Empress of Australia* would be one of the first ships to be dealt with. At the same time it was made known that when she returned to service she would be transferred to the Atlantic—the ocean for which she was originally intended.

The *Australia* made her last trans-Pacific sailing from Vancouver in May of 1926. It was her twenty-first voyage outward, for she had completed a score of round trips to the Orient during her somewhat checkered career of just under four years. Captain Hailey took her on to Great Britain by way of the Mediterranean, and there delivered her to the Fairfield Company at Govan, where her new engines and boilers were to be installed.

6.

The name of John Johnson will be familiar to few outside shipping circles, but his name looms large in the later history of the *Empresses*. Johnson came on the scene about 1924, when he was appointed chief superintendent engineer of the Canadian Pacific fleet. At that time the Diesel engine seemed to be sweeping all before it, and the opinion was becoming general that it would only be a matter of time before it displaced steam even in the largest and fastest liners. Johnson, however, believed that steam propulsion still had great advantages, and that the efficiency of steam engines and boilers could be increased to such a degree that they would continue to be much the most economical machinery for the various types of ships in which the Canadian Pacific was interested.[43]

His first experiments were made in some of the older ships in the Atlantic service. The changes made were relatively small, but they were successful, and they convinced Johnson that he was on the right track. More important, they also convinced the company, and Johnson had the unparalleled good fortune to have the Canadian Pacific's large existing fleet and even larger shipbuilding program virtually placed at his disposal, so far as propelling-machinery was concerned.

Some notes on the chief technical problems in which Johnson was interested will be found in the Appendix. Here it will be sufficient to outline the developments in the Pacific *Empresses* for which he was responsible.

This outline must start with the re-engining of the *Empress of Australia*, for although the ship herself never returned to the Pacific, the changes made in her influenced policy with regard to other units of the fleet. There was nothing very new about the machinery layout that Johnson proposed — indeed, one suspects that his purpose may well have been to prove his own competence by showing what he could accomplish without departing far from current practice. The new boilers he installed were of the old Scotch cylindrical type, and the pressure was no more than 220 lb. The engines were Parsons turbines, and in place of the Fottinger transformers he used single-reduction gearing. The only Johnsonian touches were the use of superheated steam (which a good many other companies were abandoning at this time) and the introduction of Diesel engines to drive the ship's generators and other auxiliaries. By the late spring of 1927 the *Empress* was ready for her trials, and it at once became apparent that the re-engining had been a spectacular success. She developed the designed horsepower of 20,000 and a speed of over 20 knots with ease, and accomplished this on a fuel consumption about one-third less than before. When placed in regular service, she soon made an entire voyage at an average speed of 19.25 knots. From being a fuel hog and a continual worry to her owners and engineers, the *Australia* suddenly blossomed forth as the most economical liner of her size and speed in commission.

With this achievement in hand Johnson next turned his attention to the *Empress of Canada*, which had never come up to expectations from the mechanical point of view. When she entered service in June, 1922, the trans-Pacific record was held by the *Empress of Russia*, which had crossed from Yokohama to William Head at an average speed of 19.86 knots. A year passed before the *Canada* improved upon this, and it was not until June 17, 1923, that Captain Hailey brought her to William Head with a new record to her credit. Her time from Yokohama was 8 days 10 hours and 53 minutes, and her average speed 20.6 knots. Her best day's run was made at 21.2 knots.[44]

It was not a very resounding victory, and this was made apparent in July of 1924, when the *Empress of Asia*, with Captain Douglas in command, completed a passage in 8 days 14 hours and 48 minutes, at an average speed of 20.2 knots.[45] This was the fastest run ever made by either the *Empress of Asia* or the *Empress of Russia*, and it left the *Empress of Canada* in possession of her laurels by the very narrow margin of two-fifths of a knot. In spite of this, the *Canada* showed little sign of being able to improve on her record, and, quite as important, her fuel bills continually reminded the company that her oil consumption was very high — some 225 tons per day, as compared with only 142 tons for the re-engined *Empress of Australia*, in which comparable power was developed.

A careful study of the ship's performance led to the conclusion that the fault lay in her engines rather than in her boilers. Few of the double-reduction geared turbines installed in 1919 to 1925 proved very satisfactory, and those in the *Empress of Canada* were no exception. Johnson proposed to remove them and replace them with single-reduction geared turbines of the type that had been so successful in the *Empress of Australia*. The official announcement that the change would be made came in the spring of 1928, and on November 1 the *Empress* sailed from Vancouver on a voyage that took her first to the Orient, and thence to Great Britain and her birthplace, the Fairfield yard at Govan.

As the departure of the *Empress of Australia* had already reduced the Pacific *Empress* fleet to three ships, a substitute had to be found for the *Empress of Canada* while she was under refit. This problem was solved by temporarily transferring the *Empress of France* from the trans-Atlantic run to the Pacific. Originally the *Alsatian*, of the Allan Line, the *Empress of France* had served with distinction as an auxiliary cruiser throughout the First World War, and in recent years had become widely known as a cruise ship. She was completed in 1913, the same year as the *Empress of Russia* and *Empress of Asia*, and was a most satisfactory running-mate for them. Her length overall was 600 feet, and her gross tonnage 18,481. The year before she came to the Pacific she had averaged 20.49 knots on a voyage from Southampton to Quebec. The *Empress of France* met the *Empress of Canada* in the Orient, exchanged crews and captains with her, and took her place in the trans-Pacific schedule under the command of Captain Robinson.

Work on the *Empress of Canada* proceeded apace, and the re-engining was completed within nine months. The old turbines had never developed much more than 24,000 horsepower, but Johnson was confident that the original boilers, to which he added superheaters, would be able to produce sufficient steam to drive new turbines intended to develop 26,000 horsepower throughout a trans-Pacific voyage, and as much as 29,000 horsepower for short periods. His expectations were fulfilled, and the *Empress* worked up to 22.4 knots on her trials. She then made a round voyage to Quebec which was really in the nature of an extended sea trial. The results were highly satisfactory, for on the east-bound crossing she averaged 20.53 knots and burned only 175 tons of oil per day, whereas on her record run across the Pacific, when powered by her old engines, she had burned no less than 284 tons per day to maintain an average of 20.6 knots.[46] Johnson had thus increased her normal service speed until it equalled her old maximum service speed, and at the same time had reduced her fuel consumption by more than 100 tons per day — surely a remarkable achievement.

In the re-engined *Empress of Canada*, as in the *Empress of Australia*, Johnson installed Diesel engines to run the ship's auxiliaries. Financially the change was doubtless a success, but the *Canada's* steam-minded engineers disliked the Diesels cordially. Visitors to her engine-room were sure to hear remarks about the unending clatter of the Diesels, and the tinkering sort of attention they seemed always to be requiring.

Empress of France: entering Vancouver Harbour.

The *Empress's* refit extended to her passenger accommodation, where many minor improvements were carried out. Amongst other things her first-class lounge was made much more spacious and attractive, and many of her cabins were provided with shower-baths. She returned to the Pacific a better ship in almost every respect than she had left it, though time was to show that even re-engining had not solved all her mechanical difficulties. To the end of her days she was plagued with minor troubles, including leaks in her steam-pipes, the layout of which seems to have been needlessly complicated. Few of these difficulties were serious, and they very rarely delayed the ship, but they added an annoying touch of uncertainty and discomfort to the lives of the men who were responsible for her.

Empress of Canada: Private Dining Room.

Empress of Canada: Fireplace in Smoking Lounge.

Empress of Canada: Dining Room.

Empress of Canada : Card Room.

Empress of Canada: First Class Twin Cabin.

Empress of Canada: Main Lounge.

Empress of Canada: Gymnasium.

Empress of Canada: Tourist Lounge.

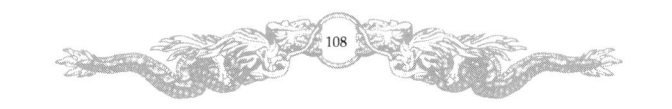

The banner on the upper left promotes the C.P.R. ships as being "The newest, the fastest, the best......................."

The fan on the upper right lists passage times to Hong Kong, Shanghai and across the Pacific.

Collection: Dr. Wallace B. Chung.

Open 3rd. Class Accomodation on the *Empress of Asia* and *Empress of Russia*.

1.) Dining Hall
2.) Open Bed Room
3.) Open Bed Room
4.) Lounge
5.) General C.P.R. promotion
6.) Daily Meals
7.) 3rd. Class Dining Room on *Empress of Canada*

As if to prove that the jinx had not been broken, the *Empress* suffered misfortune even before she returned to her regular run. In September, 1929, she made a voyage from Southampton to New York, and then proceeded to Vancouver by way of the Panama Canal. It was foggy when she entered the Strait of Juan de Fuca, and the Atlantic captain in command was unfamiliar with local conditions and, it seems, none too willing to accept advice. The result was that he ran the *Empress* hard ashore near the William Head quarantine station. The date was Sunday, October 13.

The ship lay in an exposed position, and a change in the weather might have spelled disaster. Fortunately it remained calm, and the tugs and salvage craft that rushed to the *Canada's* assistance succeeded in refloating her after 52 hours of anxious effort. She was taken at once to the big graving-dock at the Esquimalt naval base, which had been completed two years before, and there repaired by Yarrows, Limited. The damage to her hull was found to extend over a length of 145 feet, and of twenty plates that had to be taken off, fifteen had to be renewed.[47]

Empress of Canada: ashore near the William Head Quarantine Station.

The *Empress of France* was in Vancouver when the *Canada* ran aground, the intention being that the ships should exchange crews there, and so permit the *Empress of France* to return promptly to the Atlantic by way of Panama. When the *Canada* was disabled, the *Empress of France* sailed for the Orient in her stead. Fast work on the part of Yarrows' workmen enabled the *Canada* to get to sea on November 3, and by sailing directly to Hong Kong, she was able to catch up with the *Empress of France* there, and so keep the disruption of schedules to a minimum.

The marked improvement in the performance of the *Empress of Canada* brought about by her new engines soon became apparent. On her second homeward voyage from Yokohama she averaged 20.44 knots, or only a fraction of a knot less than she had achieved on her record run in 1923. Some machinery adjustments became necessary in 1930, but by the following spring she was at last able to show her paces. In March, 1931, she averaged 21 knots on the voyage from Yokohama to William Head, and in May, travelling by way of Honolulu, she did better still. Between Yokohama and Honolulu she attained the highest average of her career — 21.78 knots — and between Honolulu and Victoria her speed was 21.47 knots. In August, sailing from Yokohama direct to Victoria, she averaged 21.57 knots — her fastest run on the northern route. Her new engines gave her an ample reserve of power, and she could be depended upon to maintain a steady average of over 20 knots. The last two years she was on the Pacific she made a dozen voyages to the Orient and back by way of Honolulu, and the remarkable consistency of her performance is shown by the average speeds that she maintained between Honolulu and Victoria. Eight of the twelve passages were made at speeds of from 20.76 to 20.87 knots, and three others at 20.66, 20.51, and 20.25 knots respectively. Only on one of the twelve voyages did she fall below 20 knots; her average was 19.73 knots upon this occasion. These speeds were maintained with her engines developing slightly less than the 26,000 horsepower that John Johnson had intended them to maintain in normal service.[48]

When the *Empress of Canada* made her record run in May, 1931, she was no longer Queen of the Pacific. A larger and faster *Empress* had by then joined the fleet. This was the second *Empress of Japan*, which, like her three running-mates, was built in the Fairfield yard at Govan. The official announcement that a new Pacific *Empress* would be ordered soon was made in February, 1928, and the contract was duly awarded in June. Though she bore a family resemblance to the earlier ships, the design of the *Empress of Japan* represented a great step forward in almost every respect. Indeed, she had much more in common with the *Empress of Britain*, the sumptuous 42,000-ton express liner for the Atlantic service that the Canadian Pacific was building at this same time, than she had with the *Empress of Canada*.

Her length overall was 666 feet, her beam 83 feet 6 inches, and her gross tonnage 26,032. Her great width made her interior remarkably spacious, and full advantage was taken of this both in the fine suite of public rooms on the promenade deck and in her staterooms. A great palm court and ballroom extending right across the ship at the forward end of the promenade deck, an entrance-hall of reception-room proportions, and wide expanses of deck for sports were amongst the ship's features. Her extra deck, sweeping promenades, and huge funnels seemed somehow to increase her bulk disproportionately, and both to the passerby and to the visitor on board the *Empress of Japan* seemed to be very much larger, in comparison to the *Empress of Canada*, than she actually was.

The new *Empress* was the first trans-Pacific liner in which John Johnson designed the whole of the propelling-machinery. She reflects the experience he gained in the five fast freighters of the *Beaver* class that the Canadian Pacific built for the Montreal-London service, and the four *Duchess*-type passenger liners for the Atlantic that followed. Johnson believed that water-tube boilers (replacing the old Scotch cylindrical type), high-pressure steam, superheaters, and single-reduction geared turbines were the best combination, and in the *Empress of Japan* the results achieved were striking. The working-pressure of her boilers was 425 lb. (as compared with 210 lb. in the old-style boilers in the *Canada*), and her turbines were designed to develop up to 30,000 horsepower in normal service, and somewhat more, if need be, for short periods. It is interesting to note that the estimated cost of the new ship was no more than £ 1,270,000, or less than two-thirds the cost of the *Empress of Canada* in 1921-22.[49]

The *Empress of Japan* was launched on December 17, 1929, by Mrs. Peacock, wife of Mr. E.R. (later Sir Edward) Peacock, a director of the Canadian Pacific Railway. By June, 1930, she was ready for service. On her trials she attained a speed of 23 knots, and like the re-engined *Empress of Canada* she made a voyage to Quebec to make sure that all was shipshape before she sailed for her distant station on the Pacific. She was in no way forced, but the results indicated that her designers and builders had produced a remarkably efficient vessel. Homeward bound she averaged 21.09 knots, and she maintained this speed with her engines developing no more than 26,100 horsepower and with a fuel consumption of only 168.8 tons of oil per day.[50]

The *Empress* went to the Pacific by way of the Mediterranean, and took her place in the regular sailing schedule at the beginning of August. Captain Robinson was in command, and James Lamb was chief engineer. She showed her capabilities immediately, for she broke the trans-Pacific record on her maiden voyage, which ended at Vancouver on August 22. Her time from Yokohama to William Head was 8 days 6 hours and 27 minutes, and her average speed 21.04 knots. Her arrival was a gala occasion, and Captain E. Aikman, general superintendent in Vancouver, seized the opportunity to recall the career of the original *Empress of Japan* that had served the company so well for more than thirty years. The figurehead of the old *Empress* had been preserved and erected in Stanley Park, inside the First Narrows, and her bell is a cherished possession of the Vancouver Merchants Exchange. The new *Empress of Japan* dipped her colours to the figurehead as she entered Vancouver Harbour for the first time, and the old liner's bell, borrowed for the purpose, was used by the toastmaster at the banquet held on board to celebrate her arrival. When she was opened for public inspection, some 13,000 persons visited the new ship, and various seamen's charities received the thousands of dollars collected in admission fees.

By the beginning of 1931 the *Empress* was ready to make an attempt to lower the record she had established the previous summer. Her engines had been carefully broken in, and it was clear that she could easily improve upon her past performance. This she did in February, on her fourth east-bound passage, when she averaged 21.47 knots.[51] But it was on her fifth voyage that she put possession of her laurels definitely beyond the reach of her friendly rival, the *Empress of Canada*. The King of Siam was to travel in her, and Captain Robinson doubtless received permission to make the best time he could. The *Empress* left Yokohama at 3:32 p.m. on April 9 and was off Race Rocks by 6:48 p.m. on April 16. The Pacific had thus been crossed in less than eight days, for her steaming-time was only 7 days 20 hours and 16 minutes. The average speed was 22.27 knots. Her engines were opened up fully on this voyage for the first time since her trials, and the horsepower developed was 29,000. Her speed varied only slightly throughout the passage, for the day runs were all between a low of 504 miles and a high of 520 miles.[52]

This record was a fitting climax to the career of both Captain Robinson and Chief Engineer Lamb, both of whom reached retirement age soon after. Captain L.D. Douglas took command in 1932, and R.H. Shaw presently replaced Mr. Lamb as chief engineer. In their charge the *Empress* settled down to the regular round of schedule-keeping. No further attempt on the Yokohama-Race Rocks record was possible, for the ship was now calling at Honolulu on both east- and west-

Empress of Japan (II): Outward Bound for the Orient! Inset is a group of notables, the New York Yankees, heading for an exhibition tour of Japan in 1933. Among them are Babe Ruth, Lefty Grove, Lou Gehrig and Connie Mack.

Empress of Japan (II): the Palm Court with band stand and dance floor was on the Promenade Deck. Inset is the band of 1934: 'Ossie' Ospaldson at piano, trumpeter unidentified, Johnny Arnette with sax and clarinet, Les Hughes - sax and clarinet, drummer - unidentified.

Empress of Canada: loading mandarin oranges in Nagasaki.

bound voyages. It was not long, however, before she established a new record between Yokohama and Honolulu. Late in May, 1935, she covered the distance in 6 days 8 hours and 39 minutes at an average speed of 22.16 knots, and on the second leg of the crossing, from Honolulu to Victoria, she attained the fastest average speed of her career — 22.37 knots. Three years later, in April, 1938, she improved upon her Yokohama-Honolulu run by one of the narrowest margins by which a big ship ever took a record. Her average speed was 22.17 knots, and her steaming-time for the whole distance of 3,383 miles was only six minutes less than in 1935.[53]

7.

The completion of the *Empress of Japan* gave the Canadian Pacific the four liners, all specially designed for the trade, that the company had been endeavouring to place on the run to the Orient ever since the end of the Great War. Unfortunately the depression commenced just before the fleet was brought up to full strength. Its effect on trans-Pacific shipping was relatively slight in 1930, and cargo movements were still fairly heavy in 1931. The crisis came in 1932, and freight pickings continued to be extremely slim for several years thereafter. Statistics will best show how serious the situation became. In 1929 the average cargo carried by the *Empress of Russia*, homeward bound from the Orient, was just under 4,000 tons. By 1931 the average had fallen to 2,500 tons, and in 1932 it was no more than 700 tons. In June, 1932, the *Empress of Asia* actually arrived with less than 200 tons of cargo rattling about in her echoing holds.[54]

To make matters worse, it was at this same time that the highly lucrative silk trade entered a rapid decline. For this two factors were responsible. The first was a fall in the value of silk, due both to the depression and to the development of rayon and other substitutes. In 1924 the average price of silk had been $6.50 per pound, and it was still $5.11 in 1929. Within a year, however, it had fallen to $3.70, and in 1934 it was no more than $1.27. As the value of silk shipments fell, they naturally became less expensive to insure, and this in turn made the fast transit offered by the *Empresses* less important. It was at this point that the second factor entered the scene — the desire of the Japanese to divert the trade to their own vessels. Nor were they content merely to have the silk, most of which was bound for New York and the Eastern United States, cross the Pacific in Japanese ships instead of foreign ones; they wished to avoid using Canadian and American railroads as well. With this in mind the Nippon Yusen Kaisha built a fleet of specially designed fast freighters to sail from Japan direct to New York by way of the Panama Canal. The first of the new ships entered service in 1929, and by 1939 they had captured 90 per cent of the silk trade.[55]

Whether or not this new line paid its way was beside the point; it accomplished the nationalistic purpose the Japanese had in mind. The ties between Japanese industry and Japanese shipping were extremely close, and the task of securing a share of Japan's export trade became more and more difficult for the outsider. The bargaining position of the *Empresses* was strengthened by their close link with a transcontinental railway and the various industrial enterprises in which the Canadian Pacific was interested, and they retained a certain foothold within Japan, thanks to certain still-powerful export houses that had long served the company. The bulk of their cargoes, however, were carried to and from Chinese rather than Japanese ports, and the outbreak of hostilities in China in 1937 was therefore a heavy blow to their prospects. Surprisingly enough, general trade seemed actually to increase at first, but times were becoming difficult by 1939. Yet at certain seasons cargo holds were still well filled. Late in 1938, for example, the *Empress of Canada* docked with a 4,500-ton cargo, and the *Empress of Russia* carried about 4,100 tons when she arrived a fortnight later. But these were altogether exceptional figures. Taking the year as a whole, the *Empress of Russia* loaded an average of about 1,900 tons outward, and on her homeward passages arrived with an average of about 1,600 tons.[56]

With freight revenues falling, the Canadian Pacific turned to the passenger trade and sought means both of increasing it and of offering stiffer competition to rival lines. It is noteworthy that the possibility of curtailing the *Empress* service never seems to have been considered. In depression and in prosperity alike an *Empress* sailed for the Orient every fortnight. Nor was the scheduled speed of the liners lowered. They had been designed to cross the Pacific in a specified number of days, and this they continued to do, whether their cabins and holds were full or relatively empty. Indeed, it was upon the speed of its ships that the company depended in great part to see it through the difficult trading days of the thirties.

The most important change made was the extension of the service to include regular sailings to Honolulu. *Empresses* had called there occasionally in the past on their way home from the Orient, but the visit lengthened the trans-Pacific voyage by more than 1,500 miles, and ships with a somewhat higher operating speed seemed necessary to maintain a regular schedule. This was kept in mind when the *Empress of Japan* was designed and the *Empress of Canada* re-engined, and the service was inaugurated as soon as the *Canada* returned to the Pacific. To begin with, the call was made west-bound only, but the two faster *Empresses* began sailing in both directions by way of Honolulu in 1931.

The new service was successful from the start, and at the peak of the season the *Empress of Asia* and *Empress of Russia* made a special sailing or two by way of the Hawaiian Islands to help handle the rush of traffic. Even in the depression days of 1932 it was not uncommon for an *Empress* to clear from Victoria for Honolulu with a capacity list.

Another change made at this time was the introduction of "tourist" class, which took the place of the old second-class accommodation in the *Empresses*. The traveller of modest means, who wished to secure reasonably comfortable accommodation at moderate rates, had all at once become a person of financial importance to trans-Pacific shipping companies. In catering to his needs, the *Empresses* were at a disadvantage, for they had been designed in the spacious days when the first-class passenger was all-important, and the luxuries provided for him were permitted to absorb a vast amount of space. Except in the *Empress of Japan*, second class was, by comparison, very cramped and unattractive. But much could be and was done to improve matters. Public rooms were enlarged and refurnished, new ones were added, promenade space was reallocated as between classes, and even in the *Empress of Asia* and *Empress of Russia* the tourist-class passenger presently found an open-air swimming pool provided for him at the after end of "A" deck.

The Honolulu call had a further interesting result — it brought the *Empresses* into direct competition with the American and Japanese liners sailing between San Francisco and the Orient. By 1931 these opponents made up a formidable fleet. The Nippon Yusen Kaisha, which had absorbed the old Toyo Kisen Kaisha, had built and placed in service the three 17,000-ton motorships of the *Asama Maru* type, and the Dollar Line had recently completed the *President Hoover* and *President Coolidge*, sister ships of 21,936 tons gross. But none of these fine vessels proved to be a match for the *Empresses* in speed. The Japanese motorships could not maintain more than 19 knots, and the top service speed of the *Presidents* was between 20 and 20.5 knots. In a pinch the *Empress of Japan*, by comparison, could always work up to 22 knots, and the *Empress of Canada* to 21 knots or more. As a result, it was possible to operate the *Japan* and *Canada* on a seven-day schedule from Yokohama to Honolulu — a full day faster than their rivals could attempt. Moreover, they could travel from Honolulu to Vancouver in the same time (five days) taken by the American and Japanese ships to cover the much shorter distance from Honolulu to San Francisco. In sum, the *Empresses* could go 1,500 miles out of their way, reap their share of the lucrative passenger trade to and from the holiday isles and still reach Vancouver before their competitors docked in San Francisco. For travellers in a hurry, the *Empress of Asia* and *Empress of Russia*, sailing on the direct northern route, offered a ten-day service from Yokohama to Vancouver — a mark none of the San Francisco lines could distantly approach.

Empress of Japan (II) in Honolulu.

Pier B-C on February 2, 1930 with *Empress of Canada, Aorangi* and the B.C. Coast Service's *Princess Marguerite (I)*.

The Honolulu call brought new fame to the "White *Empresses*," as they were usually called. As this implies, the black hulls introduced after World War I never became popular; the original colour scheme, dating back to 1891, was restored within a few years. The first of the fleet to appear in her white coat was the *Empress of Asia*, which arrived in Vancouver, fresh from overhaul, in January, 1927. Later the same year Pier B-C, a vast new terminal built specially to cater to the needs of the *Empresses*, was completed in Vancouver. The formal opening took place on July 4, but the pier had then actually been in use for some months. In 1932 the Canadian Pacific decided to make use of the 1,150-foot dry-dock at Esquimalt for the summer overhauls of the *Empresses*, and on July 8 the *Empress of Russia* was docked, and her hull cleaned and painted. The other ships of the fleet followed in turn, and all four visited Esquimalt regularly each summer thereafter.

The service was carried on, year after year, with remarkable regularity and freedom from accident. The adventures of the *Empress of Australia* in the Yokohama earthquake of 1923 and the stranding of the *Empress of Canada* near William Head in 1929 were the only occasions upon which a ship of the fleet was in really serious danger. Some mishaps did, of course, occur. In January, 1926, the *Empress of Asia* struck and sank the small freighter *Tung Shing*, which blundered into her path in the crooked river channel below Shanghai, and in March, 1927, the *Empress of Canada* sank the Japanese collier *Jinsho Maru* in the same vicinity under very similar circumstances. In November, 1932, the *Canada* suffered slight damage in collision with the *Yeitai Maru* between Kobe and Shanghai; and in June, 1937, a sudden gust of wind caught her as she approached the dock at Vancouver, swung her about, and caused her to ram her bow into the reinforced-concrete side of Pier B-C. Fortunately the damage suffered was mostly to paint and tempers.

Plans for the replacement of the *Empress of Russia* and *Empress of Asia* were afoot not long after the *Empress of Japan* joined the fleet. In 1931, when they had been in service for eighteen years, the *Russia* and *Asia* were subjected to a careful scrutiny by company officials. Although, generally speaking, they were found to be in good condition, the report was critical of their electrical and ventilating systems, neither of which was satisfactory by later-day standards. The maximum useful life of the ships was estimated to be another seven years, and the view was expressed that it would probably be wiser to replace them within three years. The depression made this impracticable, and the now aging sisters were reprieved, refurbished from time to time, and retained in service. By 1938, however, the Canadian Pacific was ready to embark upon another great ship-building program, and this was to include two new steamers for the run to the Orient. Orders for these were to have been placed in 1939, but by that time the whole program had been postponed, for costs had risen to such a degree that it was impossible to secure any of the ships for the prices the Company had in mind.[57]

The *Empresses* wore amazingly well in their old age. They lacked private bathrooms and burned coal instead of oil, but they were thoroughly comfortable ships, and popular with passengers. Mechanically the most serious mishaps they suffered were cracked spokes in the spiders of their turbine rotors. One crack developed in the *Empress of Russia* in 1930, and another appeared in the *Empress of Asia* three years later. For the only time in her long career the *Russia* missed a voyage, while repairs were made at Bremerton, but the *Asia* was able to carry on until overhaul time, and maintained her schedule as usual. It is interesting to note that the older *Empresses* all wore their after-bottom plating thin, owing to the fact that they ploughed and scraped through the mud and sand in the lower reaches of the Woosung River every time they called at Shanghai; indeed, the *Empress of Canada* once wore a plate completely through, and sprang a leak as a consequence. Extra plates were eventually fitted to the ships' bottoms to protect them from further damage.[58]

Entries in log-books and voyage reports show that the *Empress of Russia* and *Empress of Asia* maintained as high average speeds in 1938 — their last complete year of peace-time service — as they had done when brand new in 1913. On the six voyages she made in 1938 from Yokohama to Race Rocks, the average speed of the *Empress of Asia* only varied from 18.34 to 18.96 knots, and the performance of the *Empress of Russia* was on a par. Five of her crossings were made at from 18.79 to 18.92 knots, while her average on the sixth passage was 17.83 knots. More remarkable still, their fuel consumption per round voyage was substantially less than it had been in 1913. The old ships were in the hands of unusually competent chief engineers, and there seems to have been a friendliness and co-operation between them and the *Empress* captains that is far from being characteristic of all merchant fleets. Everyone worked together to accomplish the end in view, and the result was astonishing. In 1939, in spite of the fact that she was then twenty-five years old, the *Empress of Russia* actually consumed nearly 10,000 tons less coal in the course of the six round trips she made to the Orient than she had burned on six corresponding voyages in 1925. Results such as these helped to reconcile the company's accountants to the necessity of keeping the old ships in service far beyond the expected replacement date![59]

8.

The only captain of the later *Empresses* who had served in the fleet from its beginning was Captain Edward Beetham, first skipper of the *Empress of Russia*. He came to the Pacific as fourth officer in the *Empress of Japan* in 1891, and had been captain of the *Empress of India* for seven years when he was appointed to the *Russia*. As things turned out, he remained in his new command only a few months, for in January, 1914, he turned her over to Captain A.W. Davison, and came ashore to take the post of marine superintendent in Vancouver. Captain Davison was a contemporary of Captain Samuel Robinson, first commander of the *Empress of Asia*; both had joined the Company in 1895. Captain Robinson and Captain Davison exchanged ships in 1916, when the *Empresses* returned to their regular run after their first spell of wartime service, and then carried on until 1919, when Captain Davison accepted a shore appointment in Hong Kong.

Captain A.J. Hailey, who had been serving in various ships of the line since 1900, thereupon took over the *Empress of Asia*. He and Captain Robinson were the senior skippers of the fleet for many years, sailing first in the *Empress of Russia* and *Empress of Asia*, then in the *Empress of Australia* and *Empress of Canada*, and finally in the *Empress of Canada* and the new *Empress of Japan*. Few *Empress* captains have been as well known, or have rivalled them in popularity. Only Captain O.P. Marshall and Captain Henry Pybus, of the old guard, and Captain L.D. Douglas and Captain A.J. Hosken, of later days, have approached them in these respects.

Empress captains seem often to emerge in pairs. Captain Hosken and Captain Douglas, for example, were opposite numbers for years. Captain Hosken joined the old *Empress of Japan* as fourth officer in 1904. By 1913 he was chief officer of the *Empress of Russia*, in which he was to spend most of the next twenty years. He left her briefly in 1914 and again in 1919 to take over his first command, the *Monteagle*, and then became captain of the *Russia* herself in 1922. He was her skipper for more than twelve years — the second longest period that any *Empress* captain has ever been in command of the same ship. At the end of 1934 he succeeded Captain Hailey in the *Empress of Canada*, but failing health compelled him to retire in 1936. Captain Douglas, a *Conway* boy who had first visited Vancouver in the sailing ship *Silverhorn*, was appointed third officer of the *Empress of India* in 1905. He became chief officer of the *Empress of Asia* in 1913, thus keeping step with Captain Hosken. In 1919, when Hosken was captain of the *Monteagle*, he was in command of the *Methven*.

In 1921 he moved to the *Empress of Asia*. Some years later, when only three Pacific *Empresses* were on the run, he gave up his command to serve in the capacity of staff captain; as soon as the fleet was brought up to full strength, he again became captain of the *Asia*. In 1932 he succeeded Captain Robinson in the pride of the fleet, the new *Empress of Japan*. He reached retirement age in 1940 and handed over the *Japan* to Captain Thomas; but within a year he was recalled to active duty and appointed general superintendent in Vancouver. From this post he retired for a second time in 1946.

Captain Douglas's propensity for happening to be in command of a ship when she made a record run reminds one of the late Captain Pybus. He was in command of the *Empress of Asia* when she averaged 20.2 knots, a mark neither she nor the *Empress of Russia* ever improved upon; he was in the *Empress of Canada* when she averaged 21.57 knots between Yokohama and Victoria in 1931, and the *Empress of Japan* when she average 22.37 knots between Honolulu and Victoria in 1935.

Another well-known *Empress* skipper was Captain A.J. Holland. (The initials "A.J.H.," it may be noted in passing, were well represented in the *Empress* fleet. Captain A.J. Hailey, Captain A.J. Hosken, and Captain A.J. Holland were all afloat at one and the same time!) Captain Holland did not climb the ladder of seniority with the same regularity as some of his colleagues; spells of service as a relief captain and a variety of shore appointments made his career a varied one. He joined one of the original *Empresses* as fourth officer in 1906, and he took over his first command — the old *Empress of Japan* — in 1919. He came ashore for good in 1931, when he was appointed marine superintendent in Vancouver, a post he held until 1942.

Captain W.T. Kinley and Captain George Goold both joined the fleet in 1913, the former as a junior officer in the *Empress of Russia*, and the latter as fourth officer of the old *Empress of Japan*. Fittingly enough the *Empress of Russia*, in which he first served, happened to be Captain Kinley's first command. He took her over in 1935, but moved the following year to the *Empress of Canada*, in which he succeeded Captain Hosken. It was from the *Canada* that he himself retired at the end of 1940. Captain Goold's first command was also the *Empress of Russia*; he was appointed to her in 1936, in succession to Captain Kinley. Within a few months, however, he was transferred to the *Empress of Asia*, and he remained in her until he once again succeeded Captain Kinley, this time in the *Empress of Canada*. When the *Canada* was torpedoed and sunk in 1943, he returned, after an interval of a few months, to his first ship, the *Empress of Russia*.

Other well-remembered skippers include Captain Herbert James, always a stately figure in his immaculate uniform, who commanded the *Empress of Russia* for a few months in 1934-35; Captain E.P. Green, who, after his retirement from the *Empress of Asia*, crossed the Pacific he knew so well in the 50-foot ketch-rigged yacht *Romance;* and Captain J.F. Patrick, who commanded the *Empress of Russia* during her last years on the regular run to the Orient.

Like Captain Beetham, James Adamson, first chief engineer of the *Empress of Russia*, had served in the fleet ever since the inauguration of the service in 1891. To begin with, his opposite number in the *Empress of Asia* was William Auld, but he was soon succeeded by W.J.P. Davies. When Captain Robinson and Captain Davison exchanged ships in 1916, so did their chief engineers, and it was in the *Empress of Asia* that James Adamson concluded his long career in 1919.

Chief Engineer James Adamson

Adamson is the great figure amongst the old chief engineers, and James Lamb looms correspondingly large in more recent days. He joined the fleet in 1899, became the chief of the *Empress of Russia* in 1916 and of the *Empress of Canada* in 1923. In 1928-29 he stood by the *Canada* when she was re-engined at Fairfield, and, when she was ready for sea, remained behind to devote his attention to the new *Empress of Japan*, which was then approaching the launching stage. He was chief of the great new *Empress* until his retirement in 1933, and was thus in charge of her engine-room when she made her record voyages in 1931. Few men knew more about turbines and their ways, and fewer still could operate them more efficiently.

Captain G. Goold

Captain A.J. Hosken

Captain H. James

Other chief engineers of the fleet who made a name for themselves included W.H. Froude, who took over the *Empress of Canada* after she was re-engined, and continued in charge of her for a good many years, and David G.R. Smith, who had been in one ship or another of the fleet since 1903, and succeeded Froude in the *Canada*. He in turn gave place in 1940 to J.B. Deans, who served in the *Empress* until within a few months of her loss.

Two further names must be added to the list, those of David Cowper and John Bald. Mr. Cowper came to the *Empresses* from the *Princesses* of the British Columbia Coast Service in 1914, going first to the *Empress of Asia*. His longest term of service as chief in a single ship was in the *Empress of Russia*, in the later thirties. From her he went to the *Empress of Canada*, just before she sailed on her last voyage. John Bald joined the *Empress of Russia* in 1913, and he became her chief engineer in 1924. About 1929 he was transferred to the *Empress of Asia*, where he remained until his retirement over twelve years later.

Cowper and Bald deserve much credit for the remarkable fuel economy attained in the coal-burning *Empress of Russia* and *Empress of Asia* during their last years in service. It is not often that ships twenty-five years old, and still propelled by their original engines and boilers, operate on less fuel, at comparable speeds, than they did when new. But another factor in this result must not be overlooked — the watchful eye of R.R. Liddell, superintendent engineer at Vancouver from 1930 to 1941. Mr. Liddell had worked closely with John Johnson, the Canadian Pacific's chief superintendent engineer, both when the *Empress of Australia* and *Empress of Canada* were re-engined, and when the new *Empress of Japan* was designed and built. He thus knew the larger ships of the Pacific fleet well before he arrived in Vancouver, and he soon made himself well acquainted with the older liners. Many of the small changes and adjustments that resulted in so great a saving of fuel were made at his suggestion, but the overall improvement obtained was due to a common effort by all concerned, and, as already noted, this effort extended to captains as well as to chief engineers.

On August 28, 1952 a gathering of some of the veteran masters of the White Empresses was held in the Hotel Vancouver. Front row-left ot right: Captain J.F. Patrick, Captain L.D. Douglas, Captain S. Robinson, unidentified, Captain L.C. Barry, Captain G. Goold. Back row-left to right: Captain J.W. Thomas, Captain A.J. Holland and Captain R.W. McMurray, former B.C. Coast Service manager, later manager, C.P. Steamships in Montreal.

9.

The war-time adventures of the *Empresses* would fill a book if recorded in detail. They sailed all the seven seas, visited innumerable strange harbours, performed an immense variety of duties, and between them made a very substantial contribution to the Allied cause.[60]

On September 3, 1939, the *Empress of Japan* was at Shanghai, bound for Vancouver, and the safety of this most valuable unit of the fleet became the first concern of the authorities. Even at that date the British Admiralty distrusted the Japanese, and the *Empress* was therefore ordered to omit her usual calls at Kobe and Yokohama and sail for Honolulu direct. To protect her further, rumours were artfully scattered to the effect that she was returning to Hong Kong, and she duly vanished over the horizon in that direction. Once out of sight, however, she swung round to the east and headed for the open Pacific. The cruiser *Kent* joined her as escort, and her aeroplane went up to reconnoitre and make sure that all was clear ahead.

The other *Empresses* kept more or less to schedule, but efforts were made to give them a coat of grey paint as quickly as possible. The *Empress of Canada*, which had sailed for Honolulu from Vancouver on September 2, had some paint on board which was applied to her upperworks where and when possible, as the voyage proceeded. The two forward funnels could only be painted in part, as the tops were too hot, but the after funnel, being a dummy, could be painted all over. The whole effect was distinctly spotty, and gave rise to reports that the ship was camouflaged when she reached Hawaii.

Late in September the *Empress of Japan* went to Esquimalt, where a 6-inch gun and a 3-inch anti-aircraft gun were installed. The *Empress of Canada* was armed the following month, and in November both *Empresses* were requisitioned — the *Canada* on the 29th, at Hong Kong, and the *Japan* about the same time, in Vancouver. By an odd chance the *Empress of Canada* had crossed the Pacific exactly two hundred times when she was taken over.

The first war-time task of the *Empresses* was to carry Australian and New Zealand troops to the Near East. The *Japan* went first to Sydney, and the *Canada* to Wellington; but the convoy as a whole assembled off Melbourne on January 12, 1940. It consisted of eleven ships, including such well-known steamers as the P. & O. liners *Strathnaver* and *Strathaird*, the *Orion* and *Otranto* of the Orient Line, and the New Zealand Shipping Company's *Rangitata*. For a time the escort included the battleship *Ramilles* and the aircraft carrier *Eagle*.[61] From Suez and Port Said, which proved to be the destinations respectively of the *Empress of Canada* and *Empress of Japan*, the liners returned independently to the Antipodes.

The second convoy in which the *Empresses* sailed was one of the most remarkable of the whole war. It consisted of the Cunard liners *Queen Mary, Aquitania,* and *Mauretania,* the Canadian Pacific's *Empress of Britain, Empress of Japan,* and *Empress of Canada,* and the new *Andes,* the largest ship of the Royal Mail Lines. Between them these seven great vessels totalled 276,918 gross tons, or an average of almost 40,000 tons each. Escorted by the cruisers *Canberra* and *Leander,* they assembled off Melbourne on May 6 and set sail for Colombo by way of Freemantle. Presently, however, fear that Italy might enter the war at any moment caused the convoy to be diverted to Capetown, where it arrived safely on May 26. Here the *Empress of Japan* and *Empress of Canada* encountered unexpected difficulties. Both ships still had many Chinese in their crews, and when the *Empresses* were ordered to sail for the United Kingdom, the Chinese refused to accompany them and enter the war zone. In the end it was decided that Captain Douglas should take the Chinese from both liners to Hong Kong in the *Empress of Japan*, while Captain Kinley undertook to muster a scratch crew and, somehow or other, get the *Empress of Canada* to the Clyde, as intended. He had his troubles, and so did his chief engineer, David Smith, who rose from a sick bed to settle difficulties below decks; but on June 16 the *Canada* reached Gourock, the seaside resort on the Clyde near Greenock, which the *Empresses* were to come to know so well.

This voyage marked the conclusion of two notable careers, for ill-health forced the retirement of both Captain Kinley and Chief Engineer Smith when the *Canada* arrived. Captain Goold of the *Empress of Asia* was appointed to succeed Captain Kinley, but as he was unable to join the *Canada* immediately, Captain Moore, of the Atlantic fleet, took command for a single voyage. J.B. Deans succeeded David Smith. The following month, on the other side of the world, Captain Douglas, commodore of the Pacific fleet, reached retirement age and handed over the *Empress of Japan* to his able staff captain, Captain J.W. Thomas.

When Captain Douglas left the *Japan*, she was busy evacuating women and children from Hong Kong to the supposedly greater security of Manila, and she completed this task under Captain Thomas. She was then overhauled, and her next assignment proved to be another voyage from Australia and New Zealand to Suez. Late in September, when she was nearing her destination, a familiar silhouette appeared on the horizon, that of the *Empress of Canada*, which had just completed a voyage from Glasgow to Suez. The *Canada* had sailed early in August in a fast seven-liner convoy that included three old travelling companions, the *Empress of Britain, Strathaird,* and *Andes,* and three new acquaintances, the P. & O. *Stratheden,* the Polish *Batory,* and the Furness liner *Monarch of Bermuda*. On this trip the *Empress of Canada* was carrying 1,918 troops and a crew of 323, or a total of 2,241 persons in all. Later her troop-carrying capacity was substantially increased, and she could accommodate 3,000 or more service personnel.

Homeward bound, the *Canada* and her consorts did not travel together. The shortage of escort ships was desperate, and the faster liners were instructed to sail singly from Capetown, spaced a day or two apart. From the point of view of the Canadian Pacific the decision was an unfortunate one, for the pride of its fleet, the 42,000-ton *Empress of Britain,* was bombed, burned, and sunk off Northern Ireland on October 26. The *Empress of Canada,* next in line, slipped through safely and reached the Clyde on the 29th. Early in November, however, the *Empress of Japan,* which had been ordered to the United Kingdom, narrowly escaped the *Britain's* fate. Off Northern Ireland she was heavily bombed, and although she suffered no direct hits, much havoc to her machinery was caused by near misses. Shaft bearings were damaged, a main condenser was disabled, and her lighting system knocked out. Working in total darkness, Chief Engineer Shaw and his men managed to keep the vessel moving, and on November 10 she crept into the Clyde, safe at last. There she was anchored in shallow water over a soft bottom, for it was feared that she might sink owing to the damage done to her main intakes. Repairs, which were carried out at Glasgow and Belfast, took about six weeks, at the end of which the company's superintendent was able to report that the *Empress* was once again in excellent condition.[62]

The *Empress of Canada* was lying at Gourock when the *Japan* entered the Clyde, and this was to be the last time that the two ships were actually in sight of one another. Before the *Japan* was moved to Belfast, the *Canada,* now commanded by Captain Goold, had sailed once more for Suez, this time in a ten-liner convoy that included the *Andes* and sundry old friends from the P. & O. and Orient Line fleets. From Suez the *Empress of Canada* herself went through into the Mediterranean,

and she spent New Year's Day, 1941, at Alexandria. The return voyage was uneventful until the last few days, when a German raider found a convoy some distance ahead and sank six ships. Fortunately the *Canada's* luck held, and she arrived safely at Gourock on February 25.

She was there a month, and before it ended, both the *Empress of Russia* and *Empress of Asia* arrived from the Pacific and moved on to Liverpool, where they were to be refitted as transports. We must, therefore, return to earlier days for a moment and bring the story of the old ships up to date.

Both of them had been left on their regular trans-Pacific run until late in 1940. The fact that they were coal-burners was doubtless partly responsible for this reprieve, for the transport authorities were well aware that it would make them difficult to man and probably hard to handle. The only adventures they encountered in 1940 came the way of the *Empress of Asia*. In February she made a sailing from Vancouver to Kobe direct, and it proved to be one of the roughest passages of her whole career. In the course of it a ventilator vanished bodily from the forecastle head, and the ship was so unsteady that the firemen had great difficulty in keeping up steam. In September a much more portentous event occurred. On the 14th, as the *Empress* was approaching Yokohama, a Japanese plane roared overhead and dropped a practice bomb that struck the ship, pierced two decks, penetrated to the galley, and wounded several Chinese crew members. Structural damage to the ship amounted to only $2,600, and the Japanese consul at Vancouver duly signed the repair bills; but the opinion persisted that the bombing was meant to be insulting and was not in the least degree accidental.[63]

The *Empress of Russia* was requisitioned at Hong Kong on November 28, 1940. She had just completed her 310th trans-Pacific passage in the regular passenger service, and it is interesting to note that she thus failed, by a narrow margin, to equal the record of the original *Empress of Japan,* which crossed 315 times. In actual mileage, however, the *Russia* far surpassed the old *Empress*. Most of her voyages were on a longer route that included Manila, and she steamed much farther on war service in 1914-18. Moreover, nearly five years' service in World War II still lay ahead of her at this time.

Her first voyage took her around the Pacific. Leaving Hong Kong on November 30, she visited Wellington, Sydney, Auckland, Suva and Honolulu, and arrived in Vancouver on January 23, 1941. The purpose of the trip was to bring Australian and New Zealand air recruits to Canada, en route to training stations, and the *Empress* was in effect replacing the well-known Canadian-Australasian liner *Niagara*, which had been mined and sunk the previous June.

In Vancouver the *Russia* found the *Empress of Asia*, which had just completed her final voyage from the Orient. This passage, which ended on January 11, was her 307th crossing, and, incidentally, the last scheduled sailing of a Pacific *Empress*. Both the sisters had been ordered to Great Britain for conversion into troop-ships, and they sailed in February, within a week of one another. The *Empress of Russia* got away on the 6th, under the command of Captain Mayall, who had succeeded Captain Patrick, and the *Empress of Asia* followed on the 13th, commanded by Captain J. Bissett Smith, who had taken over from Captain Goold. Both liners travelled by way of the Panama Canal, Jamaica and Bermuda, and arrived in the Clyde in March, where, as already noted, they found the *Empress of Canada*. They soon shifted to Liverpool, where a couple of months was spent overhauling them, installing extra ventilating fans and cooking facilities, clearing certain areas of cabins, and otherwise adapting them for the transport service.

When the work was completed, they were placed on the United Kingdom-Capetown-Near East route that the *Empress of Canada* knew so well. The *Canada* herself had sailed for Suez late in March in a convoy that included no less than twenty-three transports. Two of the Canadian Pacific's *Duchesses*, the six finest ships in the P. & O. fleet, three Orient liners, two big Union Castle liners, the *Andes*, and the new French steamer *Pasteur* were all included. The importance attached to the convoy was shown by the escort provided, which consisted of the battleships *Nelson* and *Rodney*, two cruisers and eight destroyers.

The *Empress of Asia* and *Empress of Russia* both got away on their first voyages in May, and early in June the *Empress of Canada*, returning from Suez, passed the *Empress of Asia* near Durban. On this trip the *Canada* carried a ship-load of Greek refugees from Suez to Durban, and then proceeded to Halifax by way of Capetown and Trinidad. By so doing she was able to make a crossing from Halifax to the Clyde with Canadian troops in July. The last day out submarines were found in the vicinity, and one was definitely sunk by British destroyers.

This round-the-Atlantic route was adopted for other ships as well, and the *Empress of Russia* sailed from Halifax on August 25. The *Empress of Asia*, the next in line, called at New York before going to Halifax and a photograph taken of her at the time was widely published in the press. She was not used as a troop transport on this occasion; she sailed from Halifax on September 16, 1941, in a slow fifty-ship convoy. The *Asia* was the largest of this very mixed lot, while a 1,500-ton freighter was the smallest. The occasion is historic, because this happened to be the first Allied convoy escorted by ships of the United States Navy. From a point off Newfoundland to a rendezvous south of Iceland the escort consisted entirely of American warships. No submarine attacks occurred, but there was the usual trouble with stragglers, and one ship, which caught fire accidentally, had to be abandoned at sea.[64] The *Empress* reached Liverpool on the 28th and spent the next six weeks there receiving — amongst other things — a thorough cleaning, inside and out.

By the beginning of 1941 a Japanese attack seemed to be definitely in prospect, and the pressing need for troops switched for the time being from the Near East to Singapore. The *Empress of Japan* had sailed for Singapore as early as January 12, and she returned to the Clyde on May 15. The voyage, made in both directions by way of Capetown, totalled almost 32,000 miles. Homeward-bound, the *Empress* evacuated 1,400 civilians from Singapore to Colombo.[65] On June 3 she sailed on another trip to the Far East, and this time she was to circle the globe. Instead of turning back at Singapore she sailed on to Vancouver, where she arrived on August 23. After being dry-docked and refitted at Esquimalt, she set out once more on September 30, and by the end of October she was back in Glasgow.

Meanwhile the *Empress of Canada* had had an adventure all her own. Fears had arisen that the Germans might seize Spitzbergen. As a precautionary measure it was decided that an attempt should be made to raid the island, destroy the coal mines and installations there, and so render it useless to the enemy for a long time to come. Members of the Loyal Edmonton Regiment, a detachment of the Saskatoon Light Infantry, a company of the Royal Canadian Engineers, personnel of the R.A.S.C. and a Norwegian platoon participated, and the *Empress of Canada* was selected to act as transport for the expedition. She embarked her troops on August 7, and spent the next few days at Inverary, where practice landings were made. On the 19th she finally sailed from Gourock and headed for Iceland, escorted by the cruisers *Aurora* and *Nigeria*, and three destroyers. At Hvalfjordur, the base established by the Royal Navy near Reykjavik, the destroyers fueled, and the little squadron then headed for Spitzbergen, where it arrived early on the morning of August 25. No resistance was met with, and the demolition parties were soon busy. The *Empress* was concerned chiefly with the 1,969 Russians that she was taking on board, and who complicated matters considerably by insisting upon handling all their worldly goods personally. The embarkation was completed at last, and the *Empress* left for Archangel, off which she anchored on the 29th. Here she landed her Russian evacuees and picked up a British military mission that had been visiting Moscow and 192 officers and men of the Free French forces. Returning to Spitzbergen, she spent two anxious nights there, embarking Canadian troops and taking on board 767 Norwegians. Late on September 3 — the second anniversary of the outbreak of war — she finally set sail, and on the 7th arrived safely at Gourock.[66]

This special mission completed, the *Empress of Canada* switched to the run to Singapore, for which she sailed on September 30. For a time the *Empress of Russia* was in the same convoy, but as she was bound for the Near East, she and the *Canada* presently parted company. The *Russia* was the only one of the four *Empresses* that did not visit Singapore. The *Empress of Canada* had the good fortune to land her troops there and sail just three days before the Pearl Harbour attack of December 7. The original intention was that she, like the *Empress of Japan*, should travel on to Vancouver, but she was diverted to Australia and New Zealand instead. From there she passed through the Panama Canal to Newport News, where she spent six or seven weeks being overhauled and refitted. Ready once more for service she shifted to Halifax, and carried Canadian troops thence to the Clyde in March, 1942.

Just as the *Canada* and the *Russia* had sailed in company in September, so the *Empress of Japan* and *Empress of Asia* set out together in November. This time, however, both ships had the same destination — Singapore. They kept more or less in company as far as Bombay, but thereafter the *Japan* — fortunately for her — moved on with a faster group and arrived in Singapore on January 29. Two days later she cleared for Batavia and Colombo, undamaged in spite of heavy Japanese air raids. Singapore was by that time beleaguered, and the causeway linking the island with the mainland had already been blown up.

The *Empress of Asia* was not to be as fortunate as the *Japan*. This voyage was to be the gallant old liner's last, and a rendezvous with fate awaited her in the crooked channels near the great fortress. The story is best told in the words of Chief Officer Donald Smith's official report to the Company:

The convoy passed through Sunda Straits [between Sumatra and Java] early on the morning of 3rd February. We received orders to proceed to Singapore with four other transports, the escort leader being H.M.S. *Exeter*. At about 11:00 a.m. on the 4th February, while in the narrow waters of Banka Straits, off Sumatra, the convoy was attacked by a formation of 27 enemy bombers. The *Empress of Asia* being the last in line came in for a severe attack but escaped any direct hits. Pieces of exploded bombs caused damage to lifeboats and deck plating outside the Officers Deck. The parts of the bombs and the places of contact were smeared with oil indicating same to be of an incendiary nature. At approximately 11:00 a.m. 5th February, while the ship was in a mined channel approaching Sultan Shoal, 16 miles from Keppel Harbour, and slowed down to take pilot on board, the convoy was attacked by large formations of Japanese bombers. The first formation numbered 27 planes. The two ships immediately ahead of us received direct hits and then the *Empress of Asia*, being the largest vessel and the last in line, came in for the concentration of the attack. Successive waves of low dive bombers flew over at an estimated height of 600 feet. There were many near misses from bombs causing violent concussions. Finally the ship was hit, as far as can be ascertained in three places simultaneously, the locations of hits being — forward of No. 1 Funnel, after end of Lounge dome, and through cabin No. 126 on the starboard side [amidships]. These bombs penetrated through all decks down to the Fan Flats causing casualties from the blasts and starting fires particularly in the Lounge and the main Dining Saloon. Fire parties were immediately on the scene, the hoses having previously been connected up throughout the ship, but no water was available throughout the fire service presumably due to the damaged mains. The fire spread rapidly amidships and was soon out of control, isolating the forward and after parts of the ship. The removal and attention to casualty cases, and safety of life in general was very effective and well in hand, so the loss of life was comparatively small. Meanwhile attacks by low dive bombers had to be contended with and our ship's guns, together with machine guns from the units on board, kept up a steady barrage and it is reckoned that two enemy planes were brought down.

> The ship was anchored close to Sultan Shoal with both anchors down. The bridge meantime was in flames and had to be abandoned. Captain Smith burned and skinned his hands badly. Mr. Crofts, 2nd Officer, fractured his ankle while jumping to the forward end of the Promenade Deck. Stretcher cases were lowered to the boats and later despatched to hospital. At 12:30 the ship was finally abandoned, the Commander, Chief Officer and Officer Commanding Troops being the last to leave and were taken on board H.M.S. *Danae* and comfortably cared for.
>
> At 14:30 the Commander and Chief Officer again circled the ship on board H.M.S. *Sedlitz*, then returned and organized fire parties from Naval ships and two fire floats with powerful pumps. These proceeded to the ship in the hope of saving the forward and after ends where much valuable military equipment, machine guns and small ammunition was stored. In the meantime a breeze had sprung up causing the fire to burn fiercely and the ship could not be approached . . . .[67]

Considering the nature of the attack and the fact that the *Empress* had a total of 2,651 persons on board — 2,235 troops and a crew of 416 — the loss of life was astonishingly small. One crew member died in hospital, and the Officer Commanding troops reported that fifteen men were unaccounted for.[68] Rescue efforts were led by the Australian sloop *Yarra*, whose guns kept blazing away at the Japanese planes as long as any remained in the vicinity. Her commander placed her alongside the burning *Empress*, and held her there, regardless of the hazards involved, until she had taken aboard literally every man she could carry.

A graphic description of the rescue work is given by Captain J.D. Whyte, of the Singapore Pilot Association, in a letter to the writer:

> . . . I was able to see, at a distance of some miles, the attack on the ship. As she came into sight from behind the islands she was already burning furiously, and it was evident that she would have to be abandoned. In a remarkably short space of time, all kinds of small craft began to stream out from Singapore harbour towards the *Empress*, reminding one of the fleet that rescued the British Army at Dunkirk, although this was on a very much smaller scale, naturally. These small craft did excellent service in transferring troops from the ship to corvettes and the like that were standing by. As soon as we were able to procure a launch, another pilot (Captain Gibson) and I went out to the *Empress* too. Having ascertained that there was apparently no one left on board the ship, we then commenced to transfer troops and crewmembers from a small lighthouse, where they were absolutely crammed like sardines, to the corvettes. My launch was more or less commandeered to take two naval officers back to the *Empress* to put her depth charges overboard before the fire could reach them. As I was alongside the *Empress* for this last time, her mainmast came down, but fortunately went the other side of the ship. Paint was peeling off the ship's side in square yards because of the tremendous heat inside, and small arm ammunition could be heard exploding on board. The naval officers completed their task and returned to the launch as we pushed off. However, we had got only a little distance from the ship, when the launch's engine broke down, and at about the same time the fire seemed to reach some bigger ammunition, as explosions that sounded like six-inch shells were heard from the ship. It was not long before the launch engine was put right, and the engineer needed no urging, and we left the ship altogether. By this time the other craft had completed the task of rescuing troops and crew, and all were proceeding back to Singapore.[69]

On February 9 Captain Smith, Chief Officer Smith, and others went out to the *Empress*, "but due to the intense heat of the hull boarding could not be accomplished and was postponed to a later date."[70] At that time she was still lying on an even keel, and Captain Whyte tells us that from a distance "she looked as if she had practically nothing wrong with her except that she had then only one mast."[71] Later, however, she "rolled over in the roadstead, hissing and smoking, and lay there like the carcass of a great narwhal."[72] At low tide some of her side became visible, and a small light was placed on it to warn shipping away from the wreck.[73] Salvage attempts were made as early as 1952, but the remains of the *Empress* were not demolished for scrap until 1960.

Varied fortunes awaited the members of the *Asia's* crew. Her firemen, 128 strong, were so fortunate as to get away to the United Kingdom in the transports *Devonshire* and *Felix Roussel*. Her doctor and 132 members of the catering staff volunteered for duty in a Singapore hospital, and after rendering great service there became prisoners of the Japanese. A few injured crewmen, patients in the hospital, suffered a like fate. On February 10 the naval authorities suggested that the ship's officers and the rest of the crew should attempt a getaway in three 200-ton coasting steamers that were lying in the harbour. In spite of a thousand difficulties the little flotilla got to sea on the 11th, "very short of food, fuel and charts," bound for Batavia, over 500 miles away. Surviving repeated bomber attacks, Captain Smith in the *Sin Kheng Seng* and Fourth Officer Oliver in the *Hong Kwong* reached Batavia safely on the 14th, but shortage of fuel compelled Chief Officer Smith to take the *Ampang* to Palembang, in Sumatra. Within a few minutes of his arrival there, a thousand enemy parachute troops landed on the river-bank near by, but, thanks to assistance given by the Dutch authorities, he and his forty companions finally got to Batavia on the 16th. From there the survivors of the *Empress* eventually reached Australia.[74]

With the fall of Singapore, troop movements to Durban, Suez and Bombay once again became all-important, and the *Empress of Russia* was engaged in this service throughout 1942. In June, when she returned to the Mersey after a trip to the Near East, Captain R.N. Stuart, European general manager for Canadian Pacific Steamships, reported on her condition in a letter to the company. In spite of the difficulties of securing good firemen she had maintained a speed of 17 knots, and he found the 29-year-old veteran "as clean throughout as she was kept in her normal run between Vancouver and Hong Kong."[75] On June 20 she was off again, and on the last day of September sailed for India on a voyage that kept her away from the Mersey until March 1, 1943.

The *Empress of Canada* visited Bombay in June, 1942, and on July 13, when making the usual call at Freetown on her way back to Great Britain, she had the misfortune to strip a turbine. This necessitated a two-month lay-up for reblading and repairs at Liverpool,[76] and by the time the *Empress* was again ready for service the North African invasion was imminent. The *Canada's* allotted part in this operation was to rush in reinforcements as soon as the landing forces had secured a foothold at Oran. All preparations were completed by the middle of October, and the *Empress* and other transports spent a fortnight hidden away in Loch na Keal, in the Isle of Mull. On November 1 she finally put to sea, and on the night of the 11th led a line of reinforcing troop-ships into Mers el Kebir, the naval harbour adjacent to Oran. Resistance had only ceased the day before, and Captain Goold had to take his ship into a strange harbour in pitch darkness and without any assistance from tugs. But, as noted previously, the *Canada* handled exceptionally well, and Captain Goold laid her along the quayside with perfect precision. Dawn caused a chill to run down his spine, however, for it revealed that the chart of the harbour he had been given was badly out of date. The breakwater had been greatly extended since it was printed, and the *Empress* had missed crashing into the end of it by the narrowest of margins.[77]

Virtually all the troops carried to Oran were American, and this was true also in December, when the *Canada* made a second trip from Liverpool to Mers el Kebir.

We now come to the last voyage of another Pacific *Empress*. So far the *Empress of Canada* had enjoyed exceptional good luck — indeed her ability to slip through war-time dangers, and in particular to survive enemy claims that she had been sunk, earned for her the nickname "the phantom ship." Because of this, an Italian communique, issued in mid-March of 1943, announcing that she had been torpedoed in the Atlantic, caused no special anxiety. Unfortunately the report was correct, and although her loss was not reported officially for almost a year, returning crew members brought the story to Vancouver within a few weeks.

The last voyage of the *Empress* was to Durban, from which she sailed on March 1, bound for the United Kingdom, carrying a great variety of military personnel. These included detachments from the French, Greek and Norwegian Navies and the Polish Army, 500 Italian prisoners of war, and representatives of most branches of the three British services. The passenger list totalled 1,530, and including the crew of 362 there were 1,892 persons on board.

Late on the night of March 13 the *Empress*, travelling alone and bound for Takoradi, on the Gold Coast, was about 390 miles south of Cape Palmas. There was a small moon, but the sky was heavily overcast; and through the darkness the blacked-out liner steamed at a steady 18.5 knots, on a zig-zag course. Suddenly, at 11:54 p.m., a torpedo struck the ship on the starboard side, abreast the bulkhead that separated the after boiler-room and the engine-room. It was a singularly unlucky hit, for it fractured a main steam-pipe, flooded the engine-room, and put the ship's electrical system out of commission, all in a few brief minutes. Soon after she was struck the *Empress* took a list of about 15 degrees, and although this did not increase appreciably, the speed with which she was settling in the water made it clear that she was doomed. As soon as way was off her, Captain

Goold therefore gave the "abandon ship" order, and all hands turned to the task of getting the lifeboats, rafts and floats overboard. The moon having set, the darkness was intense, and the lack of electric power to work the winches hampered the crew greatly. It seems probable, however, that relatively few lives were lost while the ship was being abandoned, although those in one boat suffered heavily when a second torpedo struck the liner under the bridge about 12:50 a.m. After this second blow she sank very rapidly, listing farther and farther to starboard. By about 1:05 a.m. the boat deck on the starboard side was level with the water, and Captain Goold left his ship by stepping off into the sea. When he was about a hundred feet away, her stern sank from sight, and her whole forward section, from the bridge to the stem, reared slowly up into the air. Then, causing much less suction than the survivors feared, the bow sank from view, disappearing finally about 1:10 a.m.[78]

An engineer's love for machinery in his charge shows clearly in the report of Chief Engineer Cowper. The first time he attempted to reach the engine-room, he was driven back by steam from the burst steam-pipe; later, when he tried again, it was only to discover that water, which had by then engulfed the steam-line, was already covering the turbine casings. In the after stokehold he found the boilers submerged in a mixture of oil and water. No. 2 boiler-room, however, "was perfectly dry & bulkhead holding quite tight." By the time he returned on deck, practically everyone seemed to have left the ship, but he nevertheless "went down for a last look around." A very few moments later the second torpedo struck, and even Mr. Cowper then felt that the time had come to leave.[79]

Second Engineer James Thomson, who was on watch when the ship was struck, had a most remarkable escape. Badly scalded and temporarily blinded, he does not know to this day who helped him on deck and found him a place in a lifeboat.

Soon after the *Empress* sank, the Italian submarine that had launched the torpedoes rose to the surface and approached the ship's boats. Her commander asked for and presently found and took on board a doctor, one of the prisoners of war the vessel was carrying. It is said that he also searched for a Greek submarine commander who had been causing havoc amongst Italian shipping, but no one betrayed his identity.[80]

The *Empress* went down scarcely more than a degree from the Equator, and the water was therefore mercifully warm. This was just as well, for many of the survivors were to spend long hours in it. Chief Engineer Cowper, for example, "was in the water hanging onto a float from the Sunday morning 1:00 a.m. until ... Tuesday afternoon about 5 p.m. It was," as he remarks in his report, which throughout is a triumph of understatement, "a long time with nothing to drink."[81] Captain Goold was somewhat more fortunate. He found a water-logged boat, contrived with others to clear it of water, and then picked up ninety-six persons from rafts and wreckage. Two motor lifeboats helped greatly in the task of rounding up survivors and keeping the boats and rafts reasonably close together. Barracuda and sharks attacked many of those in the water. Dr. Miller, the ship's own surgeon, and Surgeon Lieut. Jacklin, R.N.V.R., did all they could to assist the injured. Lieut. Jacklin was last seen going from raft to raft to assist the injured; unfortunately he did not himself survive the ordeal.[82]

The *Empress* had called for help before she sank, but rescue ships were some time in appearing. Just before sunset on the 14th a Catalina flying-boat came over and signalled that help was on the way, and the following evening (Monday) the destroyer *Boreas* and two corvettes reached the scene. A fourth ship followed, and the search for survivors continued all the next day. When the roll was finally called at Freetown, it revealed that 392 lives had been lost; forty-four of the victims were members of the crew.[83]

Only two of the Pacific *Empresses* were now left sailing the seas. One of them, the pride of the fleet, was fast and modern and had proven herself to be an ideal transport. The other, aging rapidly now, was finding the going more and more difficult.

Few liners equalled the record for continuous and reliable service established by the *Empress of Japan,* which, after the Pearl Harbour attack, was renamed *Empress of Scotland.* The mileage she covered, year after year, was truly extraordinary. She arrived back in the United Kingdom from Singapore in the middle of March, 1942, and between the middle of April and the end of December she travelled from Glasgow to Durban, traversed once again the vast 11,000-mile circle represented by a return voyage via Capetown and Halifax, made a voyage to Suez and back by way of the Cape, and ended by making still another voyage to Durban, and proceeding thence to New York. The whole of 1943 was spent in the trans-Atlantic service. On seven of her twelve voyages she carried American troops to Casablanca; the other five were from Halifax or New York to the United Kingdom. The year 1944 commenced with a voyage to

Bombay, after which she returned to the Atlantic and made another six voyages from Halifax. The last months of the war found the *Empress of Scotland* once more ranging far and wide over the world's seaways. In the fall of 1944 she made a voyage to Capetown and return. Then followed two voyages that took her completely round the world. The route in each instance was from Liverpool to Australia by way of Panama, and thence back to Liverpool via Suez and the Mediterranean. Between them the two voyages totalled no less than 58,448 miles. But this was only a small fraction of the distance covered by the fast-moving *Empress*. In the course of her war service — which concluded with a voyage to Bombay and back in the summer of 1945 — she sailed no less than 484,914 miles, and transported a total of 210,068 service personnel.

Peace brought no immediate respite for the *Scotland*; the "ideal transport" had lived up to her name so well that the transport authorities were reluctant to return her to her owners. She was employed mostly on the Liverpool-India-Far East route, but twice touched Canadian shores. In September, 1945, she brought 4,100 Canadians to Quebec, and in November she made a crossing to Halifax.[84]

We must turn, in concluding the war story, to the last years of the *Empress of Russia*.[85] When she returned from India in 1943 she was taken out of service for several months and overhauled. She was by this time the only large coal-burning transport left in service, and was beset with the duel problem of securing good coal and firemen who could keep steam up in her boilers. When she was commissioned once more in July, she made a voyage to Oran and then crossed the Atlantic to New York. On the outward voyage things went moderately well, and the distance was covered in eight days. But on September 5, when she sailed for the Clyde, she found it quite impossible to maintain convoy speed, and had to put back to port. On the 9th she put to sea once more — ignominiously, as an incongruous member of a 8- to 9-knot freighter convoy. The blow to her pride was eased somewhat by the fact that she was accompanied by a well-known trans-Atlantic liner which had fallen into similar disgrace. An interested spectator of all this was Captain Goold, who crossed as a passenger in the *Empress*, and took command when she got to Gourock. This was a decided step for the better, for someone who knew the ship well was back on the bridge, but not a single engineer who had served in her on the Pacific was left in the crew.

The rest of the *Empress of Russia's* career was devoted to special assignments. The first of these was a voyage to Gothenburg, in connection with an exchange of prisoners that had been arranged between Great Britain and Germany. In preparation for this trip the ship was stripped of her armament, large Union Jacks were painted on her sides, and floodlights were arranged to illuminate them at night. Captain Stuart was so sure that the Germans would not respect the *Empress's* mission that he protested the assignment. Captain Goold, on the other hand, accepted the voyage as just another wartime job. The *Russia*, loaded with German prisoners, sailed from Gourock at dusk on October 14, and was joined presently by the hospital ship *Atlantis*. Together the two vessels sailed around Scotland and across the North Sea to the approaches to the Skager Rak, where, on the morning of the 18th, a German minesweeper met them and guided them through the first minefields. At noon another sweeper took over and the ships continued on until evening, when they were asked to anchor for the night. At daylight they proceeded once more, and presently entered Swedish waters, where a Swedish naval officer boarded the *Empress* to help navigate her into Gothenburg, where she arrived in the afternoon.

There she was host to many visitors, including the Crown Prince of Sweden and the British Minister, but what those on board will never forget is the welcome she received from the British prisoners of war she was to carry back to Great Britain. The Swedish liner *Drottningholm* was to assist in transporting the British prisoners, and on the morning of October 21 the *Drottningholm*, *Atlantis* and *Empress of Russia* set sail. Having been escorted through the minefields as before, the *Empress* and the *Drottningholm* anchored off Leith on October 25, where their passengers were ferried ashore. The *Atlantis*, with her bedridden patients, sailed on to Liverpool.[86]

The *Empress of Russia* was assigned next to the Iceland service, and between November, 1943, and April, 1944, she made six voyages to Hvalfjordur, and a seventh to the Faroe Islands. She was in effect a Royal Air Force ship, and her passengers were mostly R.A.F. details. By this time Captain Goold had come to consider a speed of 15 knots a good performance, which meant that the engines were developing only about half their normal service power. This made things awkward, for the *Empress* frequently travelled light, and when heavy weather was encountered she was most difficult to handle. Once Captain Goold found himself virtually helpless, drifting in a savage gale off a lee shore, and it was with the utmost difficulty that he worked the ship clear. Yet, in spite of everything, the old liner continued to be a comfortable sea-boat. Service people always like her, once they got to sea in her.

After her last trip to Iceland the *Empress* was sent to an anchorage in the Gareloch, which joins the Clyde estuary opposite Greenock. She was kept coaled and ready for duty at short notice, and a call was not long in coming. The battleship *Royal Sovereign* and a number of other warships were being transferred to Russia, and in May the *Empress* was sent around to Rosyth naval base, in the Firth of Forth, to act as an accommodation ship for the Russian sailors who were arriving to man them. This required one small structural alteration — the wooden tops of her steel masts had to be removed to enable her to pass under the Forth Bridge.

The *Russia* lay at Rosyth from early May until the first of June. Then, after another short period of inactivity in the Clyde, she was brought to Lee-on-Solent, a few miles from Portsmouth, early in July. There she took the place of her old friend the Canadian-Australasian liner *Aorangi*, which had been acting as a depot ship. The *Empress* served first as a tug control ship for the great Normandy invasion, which was then in progress, and thereafter as a depot ship and advanced repair base for the destroyer flotillas. Her interior was, of course, much altered to fit her for these new duties, upon which she was employed until the first week of October.

Out of a job once more, the *Empress* was first dry-docked at Southampton and then taken back to the familiar anchorage in the Gareloch. There she lay in idleness for seven months, and it seemed as if her career might have come to a close. But one more adventure awaited her. When the war in Europe ended, thousands of dependents of Canadian servicemen clamoured for transportation to Canada, and early in June, 1945, the *Empress of Russia* was sent to the vast Vickers-Armstrong ship-building yard at Barrow-in-Furness, there to be overhauled and refitted to carry soldiers' wives and children across the Atlantic.

By September the work was nearing completion. The old liner's turbines, in service thirty-two years, were found to be in passably good condition. Her boilers were her weak spot, but these were under repair. The rebuilt passenger accommodation required only the finishing touches. In another three weeks the *Empress* would have been ready for sea. But a refit is always a particularly hazardous time in the life of a big steamer, and this was no exception. About 2:30 on the morning of September 8, fire broke out on board. Quickly out of control, it swept through the centre part of the ship, consuming it completely, and before it was extinguished it was creeping down the staircases to deck "B," where the old first-class dining saloon had been cut up into a series of family rooms. By the end of the day the liner, in Captain Stuart's phrase, presented "a scene of complete destruction," and to make matters worse two lives had been lost — those of an electrician and an engineer. Nor did anxiety end when the flames were brought under control. So much water had been pumped into the *Empress* at upper deck levels that she was in danger of capsizing. As she was lying under the big crane at the Vickers-Armstrong fitting-out berth, this would have been a very inconvenient mishap indeed, and to reduce her top hamper, her funnels and foremast were hastily removed, reducing her to the sorry plight illustrated in one of the accompanying photographs.[87]

As repairs would have cost over £ 500,000, or much more than the veteran *Empress* was worth, she was declared a structural total loss and sold to the ship-breakers.[88] Her last brief journey was from the Ramsden Dock, where the fire occurred, to the Channel Wall, where she was to be demolished.

Empress of Russia: on fire, September 8, 1945, at the Vickers-Armstrong shipyard.

Postscript

The *Empress of Japan*, renamed *Empress of Scotland*, was the only Pacific *Empress* to survive the Second World War. Her phenomenal career as a transport did not end until May, 1948, when the military authorities finally handed her back to her owners at Liverpool. In more than eight years of wartime service she had steamed the incredible total of 719,783 miles and had carried 258,292 troops and other passengers.

In November she returned to her birthplace, the Fairfield yard on the Clyde, where she was reconditioned and refitted for the trans-Atlantic service, which she entered in May 1950. First class was emphasized in her refit, and she emerged with accommodation for 468 first class and 205 tourist passengers, a total of only 663. During the next seven and a half years she made 80 voyages to Canada and also made nine cruises, two of them around the world. Throughout this period she was the largest and fastest liner sailing to Canada.

In November, 1957, she was withdrawn; she was 27 years old and two new *Empresses* had joined the fleet. In January, 1958, she was sold to the Hamburg-Atlantic Line, and sailed under the abbreviated name *Scotland* to Hamburg, where she was greatly altered in a radical refit. Modifications to her bow and the substitution of two broader funnels for the original three gave her a new profile — handsome in its own right, but very different from her old appearance. Tourist class travel had come to the fore, and the *Empress*, renamed *Hanseatic*, emerged with accommodation for 85 first class and 1,150 tourist. By the summer of 1958 she was ready for service, and she sailed successfully between New York and Germany for the next eight years. Then, on September 7, 1966, when she was about to leave New York, fire broke out and severely damaged her interior. She was towed to Germany, in the expectation that she could be repaired, but it was decided that the damage was too extensive, and she was sold to ship-breakers in November. It was a sad end to a fine ship that had rendered outstanding service to two owners and her country for 36 years.

There was never much likelihood that the Canadian Pacific would restore *Empress* service to the Orient after the Second World War. True, ship plans were ready, but building costs were high, and travel by air — particularly attractive on long, time-consuming trans-oceanic routes — was developing rapidly. As long ago as 1919 the Canadian Pacific had had the foresight to secure formal authority to own and operate aircraft commercially, but it was not until 1941, when it brought ten regional companies together to form Canadian Pacific Airlines, that it began to give serious attention to a possible future in the air. The idea that aircraft might replace ships on trans-Pacific routes soon surfaced, but the Canadian Government was slow in granting approval. It was forthcoming at last in 1948, and services began in the summer of 1949. All this is relevant in the present context because the first Canadian Pacific jumbo-jet to fly to Australia was named *Empress of Sydney* and one of the first to fly from Vancouver to Japan was named *Empress of Asia*. The *Empress* liners were to have no successors, but the Company intended that the *Empress* tradition should live on.

Freight service was another matter. In 1952 the Company decided to test Pacific waters by sending two of its modern Atlantic freighters to the Pacific. These were the *Beavercove* and *Beaverdell*, 16-knot ships of 9,824 and 9,901 tons gross respectively, built in 1946 and 1947. They were renamed *Maplecove* and *Mapledell*, to simplify translation into Japanese. The *Maplecove* arrived in Vancouver in August, 1952, to inaugurate the new service to the Orient. But things did not work out as expected. Both ships were withdrawn and returned to the Atlantic in 1954, where they soon regained their original names. Both were sold to Italian owners in 1963, and they were scrapped at Spezia in 1971.

FOOTNOTES

I. PIONEER DAYS

(1) The exact time specified in the tender was a 460-hour service from Vancouver to Hong Kong and a 420-hour service from Hong Kong to Vancouver — corresponding to an average speed of 13 knots and 14.02 knots respectively. Detention at Yokohama was not included.

(2) *Annual Report*, Canadian Pacific Railway, 1885, p. 16.

(3) *Vancouver News*, July 27, 1886.

(4) The *W.B. Flint* was built at Bath, Maine, in 1885 and was owned by Benjamin Flint, of New York. She was a wooden vessel 178.4 feet long, 35.4 feet wide, and of 835 tons gross. In her later years she was owned by Libby, McNeill & Libby; and, after lying idle for some time in Lake Union, was burned for her metal at Seattle in March, 1937.

(5) On Frazar see *Vancouver News*, September 4, September 7, November 7, 1886.

(6) *News-Advertiser*, June 14, 1887.

(7) It is a curious fact that no contemporary record has come to light which indicates just when the *Abyssinia* actually arrived. Mr. C. Simson, of Vancouver, remembers seeing her "coming through the Narrows all lit up and blowing a syren whistle," but does not recall the hour.

(8) *News-Advertiser*, June 14, 1887, which gives full details of the cargo.

(9) *News-Advertiser*, June 18, 1887.

(10) *Ibid.*, July 15, 1887.

(11) *Ibid.*, July 7, 1887, which gives further details.

(12) *News-Advertiser*, August 21, August 23, 1887.

(13) *Ibid.*, November 11, 1887.

(14) *Ibid.*, August 21, 1887.

(15) *Ibid.*, October 26, 1888 (report of interview with Dodwell).

(16) *Annual Report*, Canadian Pacific Railway, 1887, p. 11.

(17) *News-Advertiser*, July 26, August 17, 1888.

(18) It was said that the wide interests of Sir William Pearce, owner of the Canadian Pacific line, included part ownership of the Pacific Mail, but this was not so.

(19) *Congressional Record*, August 3, 1888.

(20) 51st Congress, 1st Session; Senate Report No. 847; May 2, 1890, 671 pp.

(21) *Ibid.*, p. 666. For the 11 months ended November 30, 1889, the figures were: raw silk, 790,791 lbs.; rice, 3,461,382 lbs.; tea, 8,600,500 lbs.

(22) *Ibid.*, p. 242.

(23) *Ibid.*, p. 665.

(24) *Ibid.*, p. 361.

(25) This would appear to be a legitimate assumption, as it is clear that failure to note the size of the cargo was quite accidental and bore no relation to the season of the year or the size of individual cargoes.

(26) *Annual Report*, Canadian Pacific Railway, 1888, p. 12.

(27) *News-Advertiser*, December 29, 1888.

(28) *Vancouver World*, January 18, 1889.

(29) There would appear to be a story behind the scenes in this connection, for as early as November, 1887, Van Horne announced in Vancouver that "three grand new steamers" had been ordered for the trans-Pacific trade from the Fairfield Yard. See *News-Advertiser*, December 1, December 23, 1887.

(30) In September, 1890, the *Mongkut* arrived from China to replace the *Danube*, which had been purchased by the Canadian Pacific Navigation Co. Early in 1891 the Canadian Pacific Railway withdrew from the coast trade and the Portland flour shipments were handled thereafter by the Union Steamship Company.

(31) *News-Advertiser*, April 28, 1891.

(32) *Ibid.*, August 21, 1891.

(33) These details are from the log-books of James R. Meston, who was Engineer of the *Victoria* at the time.

(34) See, for example, *Pacific Marine Review*, April 1904, p. 22.

(35) From the diary of Marshall McGinitie, who was on board.

(36) From the records of Lloyd's Register of Shipping, London.

II. EMPRESS TO THE ORIENT

(1) For the history of the chartered service see W. Kaye Lamb, "The Pioneer Days of the Trans-Pacific Service: 1887-1891," in *British Columbia Historical Quarterly*, I. (1937), pp. 143-164.

(2) Vancouver *News-Advertiser*, December 1, 1887.

(3) *Ibid.*, December 23, 1887; *Engineering* (London), 44 (1887), pp. 512, 676.

(4) The exact terms may be of interest, as a matter of record. The time in transit was not to exceed 684 hours in April-November, or 732 hours in December-March; a penalty of £500 was imposed if a boat or train failed to start on time, and a further £100 was to be paid for each additional twenty-four hours of delay. The penalty for late arrival was £100 for each twelve hours.

(5) See the article in *Engineering,* 48 (1889), p. 497.

(6) It is interesting to note that the finest coastal steamers later built by the Canadian Pacific had a gross tonnage almost as great as that of the first *Empresses,* and exceeded them in cost. The 5,875-ton *Princess Kathleen,* for example, cost $1,258,000. (*Report of the Royal Commission to inquire into Railways and Transportation in Canada,* Ottawa, 1932, p. 26.)

(7) David Jones, "A Ship by Any Other Name," *Propellor,* Winter 1986, p. 4-5.

(8) See the amusing account in the *News-Advertiser,* December 24, 1890.

(9) M. McD. Duff to W. Kaye Lamb, December 29, 1939.

(10) Mr. Duff wrote to Van Horne on April 26, 1913, and Sir William returned the letter after adding the marginal note quoted. Mr. Duff kindly presented a photostat of the letter to the Provincial Archives.

(11) *The Times,* London, December 15, 1890.

(12) *Engineering,* 51 (1891), p. 433.

(13) From a memorandum prepared by J.E. Macrae for the writer in 1938.

(14) The details in this and the preceding paragraph are mostly from the reports made by Captain Marshall and the other officers to the Company.

(15) A complete and amusing account of the banquet was contributed to the Vancouver *Province* some years ago by the late R.E. Gosnell.

(16) Vancouver *News-Advertiser,* April 29, 1891.

(17) *Hansard's Parliamentary Debates,* III., 353 (1891), p. 690.

(18) Details from the reports of the officers to the Company; also Vancouver *News-Advertiser,* June 24, 1891.

(19) *Engineering,* 52 (1891), p. 67.

(20) This paragraph is based on the reports to the Company.

(21) See Victoria *Colonist,* June 28, 1892.

(22) For a full account of the fire by Sir Edwin Arnold, who was a passenger, see Vancouver *News-Advertiser,* August 26, 1892.

(23) *Ibid.,* September 7, 1894.

(24) *Ibid.,* August 18, 1894.

(25) *Ibid.,* December 3, 1891.

(26) For a detailed account see the column-length article in the New York *Herald,* September 3, 1891; also *ibid.,* September 9, and *The Times,* London, September 12, 1891.

(27) Further details of this run are given in the appendix. In 1936 Captain Pybus, in conversation with the writer, paid a warm tribute to Chief Engineer Murphy: "I sent for him and asked him what he could do, and he said he would do his best. Then I sent for the chief stoker, Chinese, and told him, too. They did their best, certainly."

(28) Based on the records of the *Empress of India* and on an account by the correspondent of the San Francisco *Daily Report,* reprinted in the Vancouver *World,* March 16, 1896.

(29) Shaughnessy's statement is quoted at length in the Vancouver *Province,* July 31, 1899.

(30) See appendix for details and the source of these figures.

(31) Vancouver *News-Advertiser,* October 20, 1897.

(32) See traffic statistics in appendix.

(33) Quoted in J. Murray Gibbon, *Steel of Empire,* Toronto, 1935, p. 336.

(34) Vancouver *Province,* November 12, 1902.

(35) The first large shipment was made in 1903. See Vancouver *Province,* August 20, 1903.

(36) *Annual Report,* Canadian Pacific Railway, 1891, p. 9.

(37) *Ibid.,* 1893, p. 10.

(38) *Ibid.,* 1894, p. 11.

(39) *Ibid.,* 1895, p. 9.

(40) Gibbon, *op. cit.,* p. 336.

(41) *Annual Report,* Canadian Pacific Railway, 1893, pp. 10-11.

(42) The distance in a direct line was 32 miles, but 40 miles of cable were required. Laying commenced at 5 a.m. and was completed about 10:30 p.m.

(43) "We arrived at the Skagway dock just in time to receive the gang of murderers — men and women — as the citizens rounded them up, after the shooting . . . The crowd were driven into our ship with rifles behind them, with no money, the men working in the bunkers to make enough money to get a meal when they got ashore in Vancouver." (Letter from Walter Lewin, who was an engineer in the *Tartar,* to J.A. Heritage, January 25, 1940.)

(44) To be exact, $297,336.28. (*Annual Report,* Canadian Pacific Railway, 1897, p. 26.)

(45) Captain A. W. Davison described this incident to the writer.

(46) Vancouver *News-Advertiser*, October 20, 1897, which quotes his statement at some length.

(47) *Annual Report*, Canadian Pacific Railway, 1901, p. 8.

(48) The exact sum was $3,979,114.37. *Annual Report of the Pacific Mail Steamship Co. for the year ending April 30th, 1903*, p. 8.

(49) Victoria *Times*, May 26, 1906.

(50) For an account of the accident see Victoria *Times*, November 7, 1900. The finding of the Admiralty Court is printed in full in the *Times*, April 20, 1901.

(51) Vancouver *Province*, August 18, 1903.

(52) The *Empress's* own water-soaked dynamo could not be repaired in time for her sailing, and the substitute secured had proven unequal to its task by the time the liner reached Victoria. The *Tartar* was in Esquimalt dry-dock, after her collision with the *Charmer*, and her dynamo was hastily installed in the *Empress* overnight.

(53) Victoria *Times*, January 23, 1907.

(54) *Ibid.*, July 25, 1907.

(55) *Annual Report*, Canadian Pacific Railway, 1907, p. 8.

(56) The contract time from Liverpool to Hong Kong, via Quebec or Rimouski, was 818 hours; via Halifax or St. John, 853 hours.

(57) The first *Empress* to arrive with wireless was the *Empress of China*, which reached Victoria on May 29, 1909. R.L. Stevens was her first operator. See Victoria *Times*, March 12 and May 31, 1909.

(58) The finding is quoted in the Victoria *Colonist*, September 6, 1911.

(59) Frank C. Bowen, *History of the Canadian Pacific Line*, London, 1928, p. 113.

(60) Entries in the reports of the Company for 1912, 1913 and 1914, indicate that the cost of the two liners was $5,005,738.84.

(61) Victoria *Times*, August 15, 1914.

(62) *Ibid.*, December 16, 1914.

(63) *Annual Report*, Canadian Pacific Railway, 1915, p. 11.

(64) Most of the details given in this and the preceding paragraph were given to the writer by Captain Hailey.

(65) Scindia Steam Navigation Co. to the writer, November 4, 1939.

(66) On the war service of the *Empress of Japan* see the illustrated article, based on data secured from Captain Hopcraft, in the Victoria *Colonist*, December 23, 1915.

(67) Bowen, *op. cit.*, pp. 186-187.

III. EMPRESS ODYSSEY

(1) For an account of the original *Empress* liners and a history of the trans-Pacific service generally to 1913 see W. Kaye Lamb, "Empress to the Orient," *British Columbia Historical Quarterly*, IV (1940), pp. 29-50, 79-110.

(2) See S. Terano and C. Shiba, "Remarks on the design and service performance of the Transpacific liners *Tenyo Maru* and *Chiyo Maru*," in *Transactions*, Institution of Naval Architects, LIII (1911), part 2, pp. 185, 192.

(3) Details given to the writer by Mr. W.D. McLaren, Vancouver.

(4) Victoria *Colonist*, July 16, 1911.

(5) Vancouver *World*, September 12, 1911.

(6) *Ibid.*, October 4, 1911.

(7) When the *Empresses* were new, Canadian Pacific publicity booklets stated in their enthusiasm that their displacement was 30,625 tons, but this was far beyond any figure ever reached in actual service. One *Empress* skipper, when consulted on the point, suggested playfully that it must represent the displacement of the vessels when they were totally submerged!

(8) For a detailed account of the *Minnesota*, which was withdrawn from the trans-Pacific run in 1915, see W. Kaye Lamb, "The Trans-Pacific Venture of James J. Hill: A History of the Great Northern Steamship Company," *American Neptune*, III (1943), pp. 185-204. A sister ship, the *Dakota*, was wrecked near Yokohama in 1907.

(9) It is interesting to note that the first merchant steamers of any size to have cruiser sterns were built for service on the coast of British Columbia. These were the *Prince George* and *Prince Rupert*, completed at Newcastle in 1910 for the Grand Trunk Pacific Railway. Dr. Hillhouse was an enthusiastic advocate of the new type of stern and stated his views in a paper entitled "The Cruiser Stern in Merchant Ships," published in the *Shipbuilding and Shipping Record*, XIV (1919), pp. 737, 738.

(10) The best general description of the *Empresses*, complete with profile, deck plans, and interior views, is probably that in the *Shipbuilder*, IX (1913), pp. 122-130.

(11) Details will be found in the report on subsidized steamship services included in the annual report of the Department of Trade and Commerce.

(12) Dates, etc., are quoted from the official records in the files of Canadian Pacific Steamships Limited, Montreal.

(13) To be exact, $5,005,738.84. See entries in the *Annual Report* of the Canadian Pacific Railway, 1912, 1913 and 1914. The cost of the liners had first been estimated at £ 440,000 each. As the total given indicates, they actually cost about £ 515,000 each.

(14) Detail from the official records in the office of Canadian Pacific Steamships Limited, and from data in the possession of Mr. W.D. McLaren, Vancouver, who supervised the trials.

(15) A fine photograph of the *Empress,* taken while she was coaling at Nagasaki, hung for years in the office of the General Superintendent, Canadian Pacific Steamships, in Vancouver.

(16) Details from the ship's log; also Victoria *Times,* June 7, 1913.

(17) *Marine Engineer and Naval Architect,* June, 1914, p. 417 (where the length of the voyage is incorrectly stated to have been eight days nineteen hours); Victoria *Colonist,* May 5, 1914. On her best day the *Asia* steamed 473 miles in twenty-three hours and ten minutes.

(18) Victoria *Colonist,* May 30, 1914. The *Russia's* log shows that she crossed at an extraordinarily steady pace. Her daily runs were as follows: 386, 460, 461, 466, 460, 464, 463, 452, 451, 224. During the last three hours of the voyage she speeded up to an estimated 21 knots.

(19) This account of the war-time movements of the *Empresses* in 1914 is based chiefly on the log of the *Empress of Russia,* conversations with Captain L.D. Douglas, and Sir Julian Corbett, *History of the Great War — Naval Operations,* revised edition, I, London, 1938, pp. 142-149, 302, 333-337, 379-384; also chart entitled "Operations against S.M.S. *Emden* August to November 1914." The latter is the British official history. See also Franz Joseph, Prince of Hohenzollern, *Emden,* New York, 1928, in which the belief is expressed that the *Emden* once actually sighted the *Empress of Russia* (p. 162). As happens so often in accounts of sea warfare, times and places do not coincide exactly, but it is entirely possible that the *Emden* did sight the *Empress of Asia* (not the *Russia,* which was many miles away). Even though the *Empress* was only a converted merchantman, the *Emden* would not seek to engage her; her great anxiety was to avoid damage, and she was probably aware that the *Empress* and a cruiser usually operated in company.

(20) Useful accounts of the Red Sea adventures of the *Empresses* appeared in the press when they returned to the trans-Pacific run. On the *Empress of Russia,* see Victoria *Colonist,* April 9, 1916, and on the *Empress of Asia,* see *ibid.,* May 7, 1916. Captain Douglas possesses an interesting chart illustrating the movements of the *Asia* while she was in commission as an auxiliary cruiser.

(21) See Benedict Crowell and Robert Forrest Wilson, *The Road to France,* New Haven, 1921, II, pp. 553-559.

(22) Vancouver *Province,* January 25, 1919.

(23) E.W. Beatty, "Canada and the Orient," *Harbour and Shipping,* IV, p. 209 (April, 1922).

(24) *Ibid.*

(25) *Harbor and Shipping,* I, p. 389 (September, 1919).

(26) For further details of the *Methven* and *Mattawa,* see Appendix.

(27) The whole matter is dealt with in some detail in the Victoria *Times* for May 8 and May 9, 1922.

(28) *Harbor and Shipping,* I, p. 307 (July, 1919).

(29) See Victoria *Colonist,* April 19, 1921; Victoria *Times,* April 18, 1921.

(30) See Victoria *Times,* July 11, 1921.

(31) *Harbor and Shipping,* IV, p. 60 (December, 1921), and personal notes and recollections of Captain Douglas.

(32) See for example, *ibid.,* I, p. 349 (August, 1919).

(33) *Shipbuilding and Shipping Record,* XVII (1921), p. 781.

(34) See Vancouver *Province,* August 22, 1921; *Harbor and Shipping,* III, p. 901 (August, 1921).

(35) Files of Canadian Pacific Steamships, Montreal; *Engineering,* CXIV, p. 388 (September 29, 1922).

(36) The *Prinz Freidrich Wilhelm* sailed under four different names while in the service of the Canadian Pacific: *Empress of China, Empress of India, Montlaurier* and *Montnairn.* She was used most of the time as a reserve ship, and made a voyage as a trooper to the Near East during the crisis of 1922. She was sold finally to Italian ship-breakers in December, 1929.

(37) For further details of this project, see Appendix. An interesting account of the *Tirpitz* and her sisters will be found in *Shipbuilding and Shipping Record,* V (1915), pp. 339-340.

(38) For an account of these tests, see *Marine Engineer and Naval Architect,* March, 1912, p. 127.

(39) A photograph of the ship arriving at Immingham appears in the *Shipbuilding and Shipping Record,* XVII (1921), p. 172.

(40) The late G.M. Bosworth, then general manager of the Canadian Pacific's ocean steamships, visited the *Tirpitz* while she was refitting. The story is told that he was horrified to find that the nymphs that figure in the ship's decorations were very scantily clad, and instantly gave the order, "Put clothes on them!" When he later paid the ship another visit, he was not satisfied with the changes made and issued a further order, "Put *more* clothes on them!"

(41) *Official Report of Captain S. Robinson, R.N.R., . . . on the Japanese Earthquake . . .* (n.d., n.p.), p. 1.

(42) *Ibid.* The pamphlet seems to have been published late in 1923.

(43) Mr. Johnson contributed many papers to technical journals and the proceedings of learned societies. Perhaps the most informative and interesting of these, from the present point view, is "The Propulsion of Ships by Modern Steam Machinery," *Transactions of the Institution of Naval Architects,* LXXI (1929), pp. 39-81.

(44) Victoria *Times,* June 18, 1923; *Harbor and Shipping,* V, p. 343 (July, 1923), where the arrival date is wrongly given as June 20.

(45) Her best day's run was 477 miles at an average of 20.63 knots. Her day runs were 472, 463, 469, 466, 468, 477, 471 and 445 miles. Victoria *Times,* July 21, 1924.

(46) *The Engineer,* CXLVIII, p. 394 (October 11, 1929).

(47) For details of the damage, etc., see *Harbor and Shipping,* XII, p. 494, 512 (November, 1929). An average of 275 men were employed by Yarrows on the repair work.

(48) All average speeds, etc., here cited are taken from the voyage reports of the *Canada's* chief engineer.

(49) The figure is given in the *Annual Report* of the Canadian Pacific Railway for 1928, p. 8.

(50) *Shipping World,* September 3, 1930, p. 312. A good description of the *Empress of Japan,* complete with midship section, profile, deck plans, etc., will be found in *Shpbuilding and Shipping Record,* September 25, 1930, pp. 349-354.

(51) Her time from Yokohama to Race Rocks was 8 days 3 hours and 18 minutes.

(52) All details from the official voyage report of Chief Engineer James Lamb. The day runs were 462, 518, 511, 504, 505, 516, 520, 509 and 155. On this voyage the *Empress* carried a total of 1,158 passengers, of whom 481 were in first class, 218 in second class, 135 in third class and 324 in the Oriental steerage.

(53) All details from the voyage reports of Chief Engineer R.H. Shaw.

(54) These estimates are based on the cargo returns (in tons measurement) published month by month in *Harbor and Shipping,* Vancouver.

(55) See Walter A. Radius, *United States Shipping in Transpacific Trade: 1922-1938,* Stanford University Press, 1944, p. 78, where further details are given.

(56) Estimates based on cargo returns as published each month in *Harbor and Shipping,* Vancouver.

(57) This new building program was to have included two 25,000-ton 23-knot liners for the Canadian-Australasian Line, two new Pacific *Empresses,* and a companion liner for the *Empress of Britain.* The Canadian Pacific hoped to secure the five ships for L11,000,000. Sir Edward Beatty arrived in Great Britain in July, 1938, expecting to place the order for the Canadian-Australasian liners, but prices proved to be too high, and it was decided to postpone the program.

(58) This paragraph based on voyage reports, etc.

(59) All speeds, fuel statistics, etc., here referred to were extracted from voyage reports and other documents in the files of the general superintendent, Canadian Pacific Steamships, Vancouver.

(60) Captain R.W. McMurray, general manager of Canadian Pacific Steamships, Limited, and his staff very kindly furnished the writer with as complete a tabulation of the movements of the *Empresses* during the war years as could be compiled from the records available in Montreal, together with copies of any voyage reports, special reports, etc., that were of special interest. This account is based on these documents and on discussions with Captain L.D. Douglas, Captain L.C. Barry (who served as chief officer of the *Empress of Canada* during the first two years of the war), Captain George Goold and Chief Officer Donald Smith of the *Empress of Asia.*

(61) Two or three naval ships were always in company; six cruisers (H.M.A.S. *Canberra, Australia* and *Hobart,* H.M.S. *Sussex* and *Kent,* and the French *Suffren*) and a destroyer were present at one time or another.

(62) Most of the details given are from reports received by Captain E. Aikman from Captain R.N. Stuart, European manager for Canadian Pacific Steamships, in November and December of 1940. See also the interview with Captain Thomas printed in the Vancouver *Province,* February 1, 1947.

(63) See report, Chief Engineer J. Bald to R.R. Liddell, superintendent engineer, Vancouver, September 23, 1940; also Mr. Liddell's report to Montreal dated October 7, 1940.

(64) See Samuel Eliot Morison, *The Battle of the Atlantic, September 1939-May 1943* (History of United States Naval Operations in World War II, Vol. I), Boston, 1947, pp. 86-90.

(65) A summary of the war service of the *Empress of Japan* giving this and other details appeared in the Canadian Pacific *Staff Bulletin* for October, 1945, pp. 10, 11.

(66) Details from the official voyage reports and from Captain Barry. See Ross Munro, *Gauntlet to Overlord,* Toronto, 1946, pp. 279-292.

(67) This report was released to the press on May 19, 1942 — the date upon which the Canadian Pacific was permitted to announce the loss of the *Empress of Asia.*

(68) Figures from the report of Captain J.B. Smith to the company's agents in Colombo (copy in Montreal files of Canadian Pacific Steamships).

(69) Captain J.D. Whyte to W. Kaye Lamb, Singapore, July 29, 1947.

(70) Report of Chief Officer Smith.

(71) Captain Whyte to the writer, July 29, 1947. On February 7, 1942, Lloyd's surveyor in Singapore cabled to London: "Vessel remained afloat, no evidence of settling in water, and still lying on even keel.... All structure above 'B' deck completely gutted, and main mast collapsed on deck."

(72) George Weller, *Singapore Is Silent,* New York, 1943, p. 264. The date when the *Empress* finally sank is not given.

(73) Captain Whyte remarks that this light "gave me the impression of being in the nature of a tombstone, though the authorities, of course, had no such idea when the light was installed."

(74) Details from the reports of Captain Smith and Chief Officer Smith. The *Sin Kheng Seng,* 110 feet long and of 200 tons gross, and the *Hong Kwong,* 115 feet long and of 207 tons gross, both reached Batavia on the 15th. Captain Smith reported that only the good weather that prevailed made their survival possible. "Both ships arrived with fuel, water and food finished." The *Ampang,* 118.1 feet long and of 213 tons gross, was without a chart until she borrowed one from the *Sin Kheng Seng,* just before the two ships parted company.

(75) Captain Stuart to Captain Aikman, June 19, 1942.

(76) Details from Captain Goold.

(77) *Ibid.*

(78) Details from Captain Goold's confidential report to Captain Aikman, dated May

5, 1943, and from the companion report (undated) submitted by Chief Engineer Cowper.

(79) All details from Mr. Cowper's report.

(80) See the interview with Third Officer M.D. Atkins published in the Victoria *Times*, February 19, 1944. News of the loss of the *Empress* was not released officially until February 18, 1944.

(81) Report to the company, as cited above.

(82) Report of Captain Goold, May 5, 1943; also report from Captain Stuart to Captain Aikman, April 22, 1943.

(83) A complete tabulation of those on board and those missing was appended to Captain Stuart's report to Captain Aikman, April 22, 1943. Captain Goold's report describes the work of rescue in some detail. The corvettes that arrived on the scene were the *Crocus* and the *Petunia;* H.M.S. *Cointhian* arrived later. Both Captain Goold and Chief Engineer Cowper were picked up by the *Petunia,* and both stress the kindness they received on board. Sharks seem to have been responsible for many of the casualties. Mr. Cowper writes: "The sea was pretty well infested with sharks and barracuda. A large number lost their lives from shark bites, and it was so bad that they had to use rifles to shoot at them as we were being taken on board H.M. ships."

(84) Based on the tabulation of the movements of the *Empress* and the account of her in the *Staff Bulletin,* October, 1945, pp. 10, 11.

(85) This account is based largely on the record of the ship's movements furnished by the company and discussions with Captain Goold.

(86) Sources indicated in note **85**, *supra;* also report, Captain Stuart to Captain Aikman, November 25, 1943. An account of the trip by John Watson, a crew member, was printed in the Vancouver *Province,* November 26, 1943; and a feature story entitled "Unarmed, in Enemy Waters — October, 1943," by H.R. Kendrick, was published in the magazine supplement of the *Province,* October 11, 1947. Some of the dates given in the latter are incorrect, although the author was evidently in the *Empress* when she made the voyage to Gothenburg.

(87) Captain Stuart to Captain Aikman, September 10, 1945.

(88) In December, 1945, she was handed over to the British Iron & Steel Corporation (Salvage), Limited, for scrapping. The Liverpool *Journal of Commerce,* June 19, 1946, announced that she would be broken up by Messrs. T.W. Ward & Sons, Ltd.

APPENDICES

II. EMPRESS TO THE ORIENT

SPECIFICATIONS, ETC., OF THE ORIGINAL EMPRESS LINERS

Dimensions and Tonnage

Length between perpendiculars, 455.6 feet; over all, 485 feet. Width, 51.2 feet; depth, 33.1 feet; depth moulded, 36 feet.

	Tons Gross	Tons Net
Empress of India	5,943	3,032
Empress of Japan	5,940	3,039
Empress of China	5,947	3,046

Deadweight carrying capacity, 4,000 tons at a draught of 24 feet 6 inches. Loaded displacement, 11,750 tons.

Construction

The hulls were built of Siemens-Martin steel and had cellular double bottoms. Tanks were fitted in the double bottom for 755 tons of water-ballast, and an additional 36 tons could be carried in an after-peak tank. The vessels had thirteen transverse bulkheads, which divided the hulls into fourteen water-tight compartments. Six of these bulkheads had no openings of any kind; the others were equipped with rapid-closing water-tight doors. The ships could remain afloat with any two of the compartments flooded. Added protection was given by a longitudinal bulkhead in the engine-room.

The *Empresses* were amongst the earliest vessels to be built with "spectacle" framing at their sterns, instead of "A" brackets, to support their twin propellor-shafts.

Boilers

Each *Empress* had four double-ended Scotch cylindrical boilers, 19 feet long and 16 feet in diameter. The steam-pressure was 160 lb. Each boiler had eight furnaces, making thirty-two in all. The grate area was 710 square feet; the heating surface 20,193 square feet.

Engines

The *Empresses* had two sets of triple-expansion reciprocating engines, driving twin screws. The cylinders had a diameter of 32, 51 and 82 inches; the length of stroke was 54 inches. The diameter of the crank-shafts was 16 1/2 inches; of the propellor-shafts, 15 1/2 inches; of the propellors themselves, 16 1/2 feet. The nominal horsepower was 1,167; the indicated horsepower, 10,000.

Power and Speed on Trials

Though the *Empresses* were rated at 10,000 horsepower, only the *Empress of China* ever actually developed that power. During her trials she developed 10,068 horsepower on the measured mile, the maximum being 10,128 horsepower. This was stated by *Engineering* (July 17, 1891, p.67) to be about 600 horsepower in excess of the power developed by the *Empress of India* and *Empress of Japan*. In view of this, the following comparative figures relating to the 500-mile sea trials of the *Japan* and *China* are interesting:

	Empress of Japan	Empress of China
Average speed	16.85	16.6
Average i.h.p.	7,400	7,949
Coal consumption	1.56	1.594

(pounds of coal burned per i.h.p. per hour)

As this table suggests, the *Empress of China* never seemed able to use her superior power to advantage. The *Empress of Japan* proved the faster ship in service, and on her sea trial it will be seen that she sustained a higher speed with less power and a lower fuel consumption. On the other hand, the *Empress of China* reached a speed of 19 knots on the measured mile, where she proved fractionally faster than her sisters.

Fuel Consumption in Service

On an average passage, operating at a speed of from 14 to 15 knots, the *Empresses* burned about 110 to 120 tons of coal a day. The following data, covering six winter voyages of the *Empress of India* between Vancouver and Yokohama, in 1895-1896, are of interest:

Voyage	Average Speed	Coal Consumption
24 outward	13.90	1,378
24 homeward	13.75	1,495

(A rough voyage; arrived 24 hours late)

25 outward	15.23	1,714

(Sailed a day late with delayed mails.)

Voyage	Average Speed	Coal Consumption
25 homeward	14.96	1,300
26 outward	13.88	1,325
26 homeward	14.42	1,245

As these figures indicate, from 1,350 to 1,500 tons of coal were burned during an average passage from Vancouver to Yokohama, depending upon weather conditions. This total increased sharply, of course, if it were necessary to make faster time than usual. Peak consumption was reached on the record passage of the *Empress of Japan*, in 1897, when she burned 1,953 tons to maintain an average speed of over 17 knots.

It is interesting to know that the *Empress of India* reached Vancouver at the conclusion of her maiden voyage with only 32 tons of coal left in her bunkers. This was much too close a margin for comfort, and on her next eastbound passage she left Yokohama with extra coal on deck, as a precaution. In regular service, however, the bunker capacity of the *Empresses* proved to be quite sufficient, but coal was occasionally carried on deck between Oriental ports in order that the vessels might start the long trans-Pacific passage with a good margin in hand.

Coal consumption on the round trip from Vancouver to Hong Kong usually totalled about 5,500 tons. To be exact, on her first round trip from Vancouver the *Empress of India* burned 5,496 tons; the *Empress of Japan*, 5,536 tons.

Record Passage of the "Empress of Japan," 1897

On this famous voyage the *Empress* left Vancouver on June 26, at 10 a.m., sailed from Victoria at 4:10 p.m., and passed Cape Flattery at 7:45 p.m. She dropped anchor in Yokohama Harbour at 1:35 p.m. on July 7. The abstract log states that the total distance was 4,270 miles; the actual steaming-time 249 hours 4 minutes, and the average speed 17.144 knots. Coal consumed, 1,953 tons; average r.p.m. of the engines, 79.91. The best day's run was made on July 1, when the *Empress* travelled 441 miles at an average speed of 18.4 knots. On this record day the average r.p.m. rose to 80.4. For purposes of the trans-Pacific record, the passage was timed from Victoria, and the run was made to Yokohama in 10 days 3 hours and 39 minutes.

All the details above are taken from the abstract log. In 1936 the writer was permitted to copy certain entries from the notes of the late Captain Henry Pybus, who was in command of the *Empress* on this voyage. These differ slightly from the log, and give the total distance run (from Victoria) as 4,237 miles, and the successive daily runs as follows: June 27, 396; June 28, 413; June 29, 414; June 30, 421; July 1 [record day's run], 441; July 3, 433; July 4, 432; July 5, 429; July 6, 417; July 7, 415; July 7, p.m., 26 miles; total 4,237 miles.

1. SPECIFICATIONS OF THE *ATHENIAN, TARTAR* AND *MONTEAGLE*

The *Athenian* was built in 1882 by Messrs. Aitken & Mansel, at Whiteinch, near Glasgow, for the mail service of the Union Line between England and South Africa. She was an iron, single-screw steamer, and was fitted originally with compound engines of some 3,200 indicated horsepower, which gave her a speed on trial of slightly over 13 knots. In 1887 she was given new boilers and triple-expansion engines, which developed 4,600 horsepower and increased her speed on trial to 14.76 knots. The new engines were so much more economical than the old that her fuel consumption was lower than before, in spite of the marked increase in both power and speed. When first she came to the Pacific the *Athenian* had very high topmasts, but these were cut down later to the height shown in the accompanying photograph.

The *Tartar* was built in the same yard, and for the same service, in 1883. She, too, was an iron, single-screw steamer, and her original compound machinery was likewise removed and replaced by triple-expansion engines. Captain A.W. Davison, whose first command she was, in 1905, recalls that she was an exceptionally well-built ship, with solid teak deck-rails and elaborate brass fittings. He states that upon one occasion she was used as a royal yacht by Queen Victoria, and that when she came to the Pacific the furniture in one of her rooms still bore the royal arms.

The *Monteagle* was a steel ship, and was completed in March, 1899, by the Palmers' Company, of Newcastle. She was built for the Beaver Line, and, as stated elsewhere, was one of a very successful series of cattle and freight steamers built by the line in the decade 1897-1907. Her regular run was from Bristol to Montreal, though she made voyages to various ports in the United States as well. While on the Atlantic she became noted for the consistency of her performance, and her ability to keep strictly to schedule, in fair weather and foul. Her three double-ended Scotch boilers had a heating surface of 11,721 square feet and a grate area of 363 square feet. Her triple-expansion engines drove twin screws. The *Monteagle* was the first vessel in the Canadian Pacific trans-Pacific fleet to have refrigerated cargo space. Its capacity was 24,785 cubic feet.

The principal dimensions of the three steamers were as follows:

	Length	Width	Depth	Tons Gross	Tons Net
Athenian	365.0	45.8	29.0	3,882	2,440
Tartar	376.5	47.2	30.3	4,425	2,768
Monteagle	445.0	52.2	27.7*	6,163	3,953

* Depth moulded, 30 feet 10 inches.

2. WESTBOUND TRAFFIC STATISTICS, 1892 AND 1897

Careful search has so far failed to reveal any official record of the traffic handled by the *Empresses* during the nineties. It has therefore been necessary to turn to the newspapers of the time for the statistics set forth in the two tables which follow. The arrival of practically every *Empress* was described at some length in early days. As the tables themselves suggest, the ship reporters frequently secured from the purser a detailed return of the passengers carried. However, at other times they were content with estimates or round figures, and it must therefore be emphasized that *too much reliance must not be placed on the totals given*. It can be said with confidence that they are not very wide of the mark, but on the other hand it is equally certain that they are not entirely accurate.

Oddly enough, much less attention was given by the press to the sailings of the *Empresses* than to their arrivals, and it has proven quite impossible to compile any corresponding tables for their outward voyages.

Canadian Pacific Trans-Pacific Steamships

(a) Passengers carried, Inward Voyages, 1892

Arrival Date	1st Class	2nd Class	Steerage	Total
January 26	13	8	191	212
February 22	18	1	240	259
March 22	36	22	300	358
April 19	81	22	530	633
May 7	82	8	450	540
May 28	120	11	552	683
June 18	136	—	416	552
July 8	151	—	286	437
July 29	109	18	198	325
August 25	48	13	145	206
September 9	47	14	104	165
September 30	35	8	144	187
October 30	52	18	249	319
November 22	40	7	178	225
December 20	25	6	329	360
Totals	993	156	4,312	5,461

(b) Passengers and Cargo carried, Inward Voyages, 1897

Arrival Date	1st Class	2nd Class	Steerage	Total	Cargo (Tons Measurements)
January 13	14	24	248	286	2,772
February 11	23	1	289	313	1,895
March 10	27	—	343	370	2,341
April 8	41	12	790	843	1,600
April 27	110	—	687	797	1,898
May 19	130	13	487	630	2,200
June 9	127	24	376	527	1,853
June 30	91	19	373	483	2,134
July 20	61	—	375	436	2,265
August 11	62	9	223	294	1,929
September 1	64	8	210	282	2,438
September 21	38	14	271	323	1,500
October 20	28	8	307	343	2,200
November 17	22	11	212	245	2,000
December 15	22	—	150	172	2,074
Totals	860	143	5,341	6,344	31,099

3. TRAFFIC STATISTICS, 1908-1913

Official returns of the traffic handled by the trans-Pacific steamers are available for the years 1908 to 1913. These are included in the report on subsidized steamship services which is found in the annual report of the Department of Trade and Commerce. The tables which follow have been compiled from this source.

Canadian Pacific Trans-Pacific Steamships

Traffic Statistics, 1908-1913

(a) Passengers

	1st Class	3rd Class	4th Class	Total (Steerage)
Inward voyages				
1908	706	622	6,242	7,570
1909	583	607	4,868	6,058
1910	955	772	6,086	7,813
1911	697	565	4,846	6,108
1912	394	969	5,610	6,973
1913	970	752	6,128	7,850

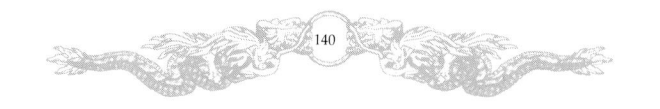

(a) Passengers

	1st Class	3rd Class	4th Class	Total (Steerage)
Outward voyages				
1908	576	245	3,943	4,764
1909	523	160	3,371	4,054
1910	623	170	3,889	4,682
1911	429	176	2,184	2,789
1912	255	361	4,059	4,675
1913	660	368	4,693	5,721
Inward and outward				
1908	1,282	867	10,185	12,334
1909	1,106	767	8,239	10,112
1910	1,578	942	9,975	12,495
1911	1,126	741	7,030	8,897
1912	649	1,330	9,669	11,648
1913	1,630	1,120	10,821	13,571

(b) Freight

	Tons Weight	Tons Measurement
Inward voyages		
1908	12,256	29,018
1909	12,659	———
1910	2,205	54,368
1911	———	23,434
1912	19,050	———
1913	26,377	———
Outward voyages		
1908	9,040	13,092
1909	14,053	———
1910	8,747	18,170
1911	———	14,878
1912	28,183	———
1913	31,937	———
Inward and outward		
1908	21,296	42,110
1909	26,712	———
1910	10,952	72,538
1911	———	40,332
1912	47,233	———
1913	58,314	———

III. EMPRESS ODYSSEY

1. SPECIFICATIONS OF THE LATER *"EMPRESSES"*

The principal dimensions of the *Empresses* are given in the accompanying table. For purposes of comparison it may be interesting to recall that the over-all length of the three original *Empress* liners, which entered service in 1891, was 485 feet, their length between perpendiculars 455.6 feet, gross tonnage 5,940, and displacement 11,750 tons. Their triple-expansion reciprocating engines were rated at 10,000 horsepower, but in actual service, with the vessels operating at 14 to 15 knots, they developed about half this total.

	EMPRESS OF RUSSIA	EMPRESS OF ASIA	EMPRESS OF CANADA	EMPRESS OF JAPAN	EMPRESS OF AUSTRALIA
Launched	Aug. 28, 1912	Nov. 23, 1912	Aug. 17, 1920	Dec. 17, 1929	Dec. 20, 1913
Completed	Mar., 1913	May, 1913	Apr., 1922	June, 1930	June, 1922
Gross tonnage	16,810	16,909	21,547	26,032	21,861
Under-deck tonnage	12,557	12,545	15,170	17,737	14,149
Net tonnage	8,789	8,883	12,811	15,725	12,292
Length over-all	592.0'	592.0'	653.0'	666.0'	615.0'
Length b.p.	570.2'	570.1'	627.0'	644.0'	589.9'
Width	68.2'	68.2'	77.9'	83.8'	75.2'
Depth	42.0'	42.0'	42.2'	44.5'	41.5'
Depth moulded	46'0"	46'0"	45'2"	48'6"	46'2"
Normal service draught	29'0"	29'0"	28'9 3/4"	30'0"	29'0"
Normal service displacement	21,635	—2	26,644	30,754	25,100
Maximum service displacement	25,200	25,400	32,250	39,000	32,800
Dead-weight carrying capacity	9,135	9,135	10,194	10,300	7,706

	Empress of Russia	Empress of Asia	Empress of Canada		Empress of Japan	Empress of Australia	
			1922	1929		1922	1927
Engines	Parsons turbines direct-coupled.	Parsons turbines direct coupled	Brown-Curtis turbines, double-reduction gearing.	Parsons turbines, single reduction gearing.	Parsons Turbines single-reduction gearing.	Brown-Curtis turbines, Föttinger hydraulic transformers.	Parsons turbines, single reduction gearing.
Propellors	Quadruple	Quadruple	Twin	Twin	Twin	Twin	Twin
Designed S.H.P.	18,500	18,500	20,000	26,000	29,000	15,600	20,000
Designed Service Speed	18	18	18	20.8	21	17	18
Max. Trial Speed	21.178	21.43	20.3	22.4	22.38	17.2	20.345
Highest average speed in service	19.86	20.2	20.6	21.78	22.37	16.4	----
Boilers type	Scotch Cylindrical	Scotch Cylindrical	Scotch Cylindrical		Yarrow water-tube (2 scotch type-type aux.).	Vulcan water-tube.	Scotch Cylindrical
Number	6 D.E., 4 S.E.	6 D.E., 4 S.E.	8 D.E., 4 S.E.		6 (and 2 aux.)	14	6 D.E., 1 S.E.
Furnaces	64	64	60		----	40	40
Pressure, lb.	190	190	210		425 (200 in aux)	241	220
Heating Surface	54,251	54,251	49,320		52,950(6)	46,280	38,075
Fuel	Coal	Coal	Oil		Oil	Oil	Oil
Passenger	1917 1921	1925 1939(3)	1925	1939	1930 1939	1925	
First Class	296 374	374 207	444	348	399 293	410	
Second Class	84 66	73 137 (4)	162	79 (4)	164 164(4)	165	
Third Class	--- 92	92 79	164	192	100 100	194	
Orientals	800 670	728 470	924	596	510 558	674	
Totals	1,180 1,202	1,240 893	1,694	1,215	1,173 1,115	1,443	
Crew in 1936							
Deck department	88	88	95		103	90	
Pursers	7	7	7		7	7	
Engineers' Department	209	209	110		123	72	
Catering Dept.	208	216	303		353	326	
Total Crew	512	520	515		586	495	

1 The *Empress of Australia* (then the *Tirpitz*) seems to have been completed about May, 1919. She was purchased by the Canadian Pacific in the summer of 1921, and alterations made by the company, which included conversion of her boilers to burn oil instead of coal, were completed in June, 1922.

2 The exact figure is not available; it would be a few tons in excess of the corresponding displacement of the *Empress of Russia*. Early advertising folders gave the displacement of the two ships as 30,625 tons, but this was never approached in actual service.

3 *Empress of Russia*. Totals for the *Empress of Asia* were: First class, 217; tourist, 137; third class, 91; Oriental steerage, 470; total, 915.

4 Tourist class, which had replaced the old second class.

5 The contract called for a year-round average service speed of 21 knots, "unusually heavy weather only excepted." At the 29,000 S.H.P. the speed would exceed 21 knots, but this power and extra speed would be required to make good delays due to fog and other causes.

6 Plus 17,730 square feet in superheaters and 7,270 square feet in auxiliary boilers; grand total, 77,950 square feet.

2. SERVICE PERFORMANCE OF THE *"EMPRESSES"*

Few liners have served their owners as well as the *Empress of Russia* and *Empress of Asia*. They met with remarkably few serious mishaps, and, so far as the writer is aware, the only occasion upon which either of the sisters failed to make a peace-time sailing was in 1930, when a fractured turbine spider compelled the *Empress of Russia* to skip a voyage. It is true that, on paper, their schedule appeared to be a leisurely one compared with that of many Atlantic liners. A round trip to the Orient usually lasted fifty-six days, which would include a week or ten days spent in Vancouver. Actual steaming time was usually about thirty-two days out of the fifty-six. But these figures are deceptive. A Pacific *Empress* made as many as fifteen calls on a voyage, and once she left Vancouver she had only fits and snatches of time in port until she was back again. The voyage from Vancouver to Manila totalled 6,946 miles (or 8,458 if the route was via Honolulu), whereas an Atlantic *Empress* only covered 2,759 miles in a voyage from Quebec to Southampton. The *Russia* and *Asia* travelled about 83,500 miles in an average year; during their last years in service this was increased to about 86,500 miles by the two calls they usually made each season at Honolulu. The larger *Empresses*, sailing regularly via the Hawaiian Islands, would pass the 100,000-mile mark in a year.

Like most ships, the *Empress of Russia* and *Empress of Asia* developed tricks that became well known to the men who ran them. For one thing, they could splash water onto the officers on the bridge with an artfulness reminiscent of the famous old *Mauretania*. This was probably because they were, if anything, a little too fine-lined forward; their sharp bows would cut deeply into a big wave, then the water would rise suddenly with a mighty surge under the flare of the forecastle and throw the bow into the air — with uncomfortable consequences for all on board. Most of the men who sailed in them also feel that they were a few feet too narrow. At the time they were built, the Fairfield designers seem to have favoured a relatively narrow ship, for the Fairfield-built *Calgarian* was 2 feet narrower than her sister ship, the *Alsatian* (later the *Empress of France*), which hailed from the Beardmore yard, and the feeling seems to be that the *Alsatian* was the better ship of the two. This is not to imply that the *Empress of Russia* and *Empress of Asia* were not successful and popular ships, for they were unusually comfortable from the passenger's point of view. The point is that later experience has shown that an increase in beam that would at one time have been considered quite disproportionate can be all to the good, and if the *Empresses* had been 3 or 4 feet wider, they would probably have been more comfortable still. It is a pity, too, that they were never converted to burn oil fuel. The change was considered seriously on a number of occasions, but the estimated cost was deemed to be excessive. The disruption of sailing schedules the refit would have occasioned was doubtless another factor that weighed heavily in the decision.

As the turbines in the *Russia* and *Asia* were coupled directly to the propellor shafts, the propellors revolved at relatively high speed. The propellors themselves were therefore small in diameter — no more than 9 feet — and, as there had to be four of them, the wing propellors were well out to the line of the ship's side. The result was that when the *Empresses* rolled heavily, a wing propellor would come to the surface, and, as a consequence, lose its propulsive efficiency for a moment or two. This gave rise to another "trick" — a tendency to swing off course suddenly in a heavy sea, when the wing propellor ceased to function properly.

Some further data regarding the trials of the *Russia* and *Asia* may be of interest. On the measured mile the results of the progressive trials of the *Empress of Russia* were as follows:

Runs	Knots	S.H.P.	R.P.M.
First	12,415	4,225	—
Second	15,211	8,030	—
Third	17,143	11,620	—
Fourth	19,278	17,310	—
Fifth	20,112	20,740	304.5
Sixth	21,178	26,285	327.8

As the design called for a speed of 18 knots at 18,500 S.H.P., it will be seen that the contract requirements were comfortably exceeded. On her twelve-hour sea trial the *Russia* averaged 305 R.P.M., and it was calculated that this was equivalent to a speed of 20.14 knots. Her mean draught on her progressive trials was 26 feet 8 inches, which corresponded with a displacement of 19,500 tons. The *Empress of Asia* proved to be a little faster on trial, possibly because she was drawing only 25 feet 8 inches and displacing 18,650 tons. Her fastest measured-mile runs were:

Knots	S.H.P.	R.P.M.	Slip
21.33	27,010	330	20.7%
21.43	27,280	332	20.6%

A slip of over 20 per cent would horrify an engineer nowadays, but the high-speed propellors necessitated by direct-coupled turbines made this result unavoidable.

It is interesting to compare these figures with the results secured in actual service. It so happens that complete statistics are available covering the *Russia's* last passage from Yokohama to Race Rocks, and these will enable us to place the final service performance of the 26-year-old veteran alongside her trial runs.

Sailing Date, 1940	Average Speed	Mean Displacement	Average S.H.P.	R.P.M.	Coal per Day	Coal per H.P. per Hour
					Tons	Lb.
March 7	18.46	19,510	17,860	—	253.9	1.32
April 26	17.45	20,382	14,854	256.8	233.1	1.46
June 21	17.50	20,120	14,130	253.3	213.2	1.40
August 16	17.47	20,325	15,860	260.4	223.6	1.23
October 12	18.01	19,530	17,300	268.7	260.9	1.40

In his report the chief engineer explained that poor coal was responsible for the high fuel consumption on the final voyage, but the fact of the matter was that the *Empress* was burning much less fuel than when she was brand new. In 1917, for example, the *Empress of Asia* burned an average of 311.2 tons of coal per day to average 18.46 knots, or precisely the same speed that the *Russia* maintained in 1940 on a consumption of only 253.9 tons. For years the *Empresses* burned well over 10,000 tons of coal per round voyage as a matter of course, but in the thirties this was lowered substantially. Consumption on six voyages of the *Empress of Russia* in 1939 totalled only 53,194 tons (an average of 8,866 tons), as compared with 62,807 tons (an average of 10,468 tons) for six voyages in 1925.

It will be noted that the two older *Empresses* were operated at a mean displacement of about 20,000 tons on an average voyage. Their regular coaling ports were Vancouver and Nagasaki. The *Empress of Canada* usually displaced about 25,500 tons in ordinary service. The oil-burning ships took on fuel in Vancouver, Honolulu and Yokohama.

So many rumours got afloat about the builders' trials of the *Empress of Canada* in 1921 that the following notes on her official trials on the measured mile, which took place on April 30 and May 1, 1922, will be of interest. All figures are from the Canadian Pacific's own records:

Knots	S.H.P.	R.P.M.
18.26	16,320	99.40
19.06	18,900	104.50
19.51	20,770	107.50
19.82	21,840	109.00
20.10	21,670	110.35

These trials were run at a draught of 27 feet, and a displacement of 24,650 tons. According to *Engineering* the *Canada* made another run at 20.3 knots and developed 24,000 S.H.P. at 111 R.P.M.

The *Empress of Canada* handled particularly well, and in spite of her greater length the *Empress* captains found her easier to dock and manoeuvre than the smaller

Asia and *Russia*. She was a good sea boat, though the opinion seems to be general that she was not quite as comfortable from the passenger's point of view as the older liners. Her one bad habit was taking water forward, and bulwarks and deck fittings were apt to take a beating unless she was watched carefully in bad weather. The *Canada's* troubles were mostly mechanical, and in later years she was plagued with small boiler cracks, leaking pipes, and so on. Few of these were of much consequence in themselves, but they were a worry and a nuisance to her engineers. Her new turbines proved very satisfactory, although the first pinions in the single-reduction gearing gave trouble and had to be replaced in 1930. Her performance in actual service may be judged from the records of her last four passages from Victoria to Honolulu in 1939. The figures follow:

Average Speed	Displacement	S.H.P.	Lb. Oil per S.H.P. per Hour	Slip
20.38 knots	25,650	25,875	0.705	10.30%
20.36 knots	25,475	25,902	0.7147	10.19%
20.49 knots	25,560	25,942	0.7037	9.41%
20.06 knots	25,530	25,894	0.728	11.14%

With her original engines the fuel consumption of the *Canada* had been about 1.13 pounds of oil per horsepower per hour, and the great saving in fuel the re-engining brought about will be apparent, especially when it is remembered that the fuel bill of an *Empress* in a year is measured in hundreds of thousands of dollars.

The engines and boilers of the *Empress of Japan* (later the *Empress of Scotland*) were designed by John Johnson, and represent standards of performance towards which he had been working for some years. The first task Johnson undertook after he became chief superintendent engineer of the Canadian Pacific fleet was the development of better condenser tubes. He experimented with various alloys, and eventually found one that virtually eliminated the likelihood of tube failure, unless caused by manufacturing defects. With this preliminary problem solved, he turned his attention to superheated steam and the use of water-tube boilers, for he was convinced that the way to greater economy lay in the direction of higher steam-pressures and steam-temperatures. The first passenger liners in which his ideas were applied fully were the *Duchess* class steamers, completed in 1928 and later years for the trans-Atlantic service. In succeeding vessels Johnson increased both the steam-pressure and the size of individual boilers, and he also raised the temperature to which steam was superheated. In the *Empress of Japan* only six boilers were installed to generate steam for turbines of 30,000 horsepower, and steam was superheated to 750 degrees. The small number of boilers made possible a very simple and efficient steam-pipe layout. In the *Empress of Canada* the twelve old-style boilers were linked up by an intricate maze of piping that weighed 9 tons, whereas the six larger water-tube boilers in the *Japan* were linked up by a simple, straightforward system that weighed only 6 tons. The over-all economy that Johnson achieved was remarkable. On her trial voyage from Quebec to Southampton in 1930 the *Empress of Japan* averaged 21.09 knots on a fuel consumption of only 0.603 pound of oil per horsepower per hour, or less than half the fuel consumed by the smaller *Empress of Canada* when propelled by her original engines. The following figures relating to the *Japan's* record runs between Yokohama and Honolulu are interesting:

Date	Speed	Displacement	S.H.P.	R.P.M.	Slip	Tons of Oil per Day
May, 1935	22.16	26,817	28,785	121.05	7.23%	192.20
April, 1938	22.17	26,965	28,908	121.40	7.43%	195.32

3. DESIGN OF THE *"EMPRESS OF AUSTRALIA"*

The *Empress of Australia*, originally the *Tirpitz*, was one of three liners built by the Hamburg-Amerika Line for a new de luxe service to South America that was to have been maintained jointly with the Hamburg-South American Line. Her maiden voyage was originally scheduled for October 29, 1914. Her sister ships received the unattractive names of *William O'Swald* and *Johan Heinrich Burchard*. Of the three, only the *Tirpitz* was fitted with the new-fangled Fottinger transformers. After the Great War the *O'Swald* and *Burchard* ran to South America briefly for the Royal Holland Lloyd under the names *Brabantia* and *Limburgia*, but they were soon transferred to the American flag and the trans-Atlantic service as the *Resolute* and *Reliance*. After another year or two they were purchased by their original owners, the Hamburg-Amerika Line, which employed them for a dozen years on the Atlantic and as cruising steamers. In 1937 the *Resolute* was sold to the Italians and became the *Lombardia*. Both ships met a fiery end — the *Reliance* at Hamburg in September, 1939, just as the Second World War was starting, and the *Lombardia* at Naples in September, 1943. The *Empress of Australia* served as a transport throughout the war, and operated under the control of the British Ministry of Transport. Like the *Empress of Canada*, she was reported sunk several times by the enemy, but happily the claims were unfounded. The Canadian Pacific announced in 1947 that they did not propose to recondition the *Empress*, and presumably she was be disposed of as soon she completed her work as a transport.

The *Australia* was anything but graceful in appearance. Her upperworks were high and bulky, deck being piled on deck in true German style. The tops of her funnels were no less than 140 feet 1 inch above her keel, whereas the corresponding height of the *Empress of Canada* was only 119 feet and that of the *Empress of Russia* 114 feet 6 inches.

4. DIMENSIONS OF THE *"MATTAWA"* AND *"METHVEN"*

The *Mattawa* was built by A. M'Millan & Sons, Ltd., at Dumbarton, for MacVicar Marshall & Company. Her original name was *Saint Hugo*. She was launched on June 15, 1912, and completed the following month. Her dimensions were 401 by 52.1 by 27.3 feet, and her gross tonnage 4,874 tons. Her dead-weight carrying capacity was 8,120 tons, and her loaded displacement 11,165 tons. Her maximum speed was 10.3 knots, and her average speed 9.5 knots. Her name had been changed to *Franktor* before the Canadian Pacific purchased her in 1916, and they in turn renamed her *Mattawa*. When the company decided to give all its freighters names commencing with the letter "B," she became the *Berwyn*. She was sold to the Kintyre Steamship Company on January 17, 1928.

The *Methven* had had a varied and interesting career before she was acquired by the Canadian Pacific in 1917. Built in 1905 as the *Heliopolis*, her first owners were Harris & Dixon. Her dimensions were 390 by 52.7 by 27.1 feet, and her gross tonnage 4,852 tons. Her dead-weight carrying capacity was 7,895 tons, and her loaded displacement 12,050 tons. Her maximum speed was 10.9 knots, and her average speed 10 knots. Her builders were D. & W. Henderson & Co., Ltd., of Glasgow. Shortly before the first Great War she was purchased by the British Admiralty and fitted out as the auxiliary hospital ship *Mediator*. Not long after this the famous old hospital ship *Maine* was wrecked, and the Admiralty thereupon changed the name of the *Mediator* to *Maine*, and used her as a replacement. She seems to have continued in service as a hospital ship until sold to the Canadian Pacific in 1917. *Methven* was her next name, and she sailed under it until renamed *Borden* in 1923. She was sold on October 26, 1926, and was broken up soon after by Dutch scrappers.

5. TRANS-PACIFIC RECORD PASSAGES, 1913 TO 1938

For purposes of comparison it may be noted that the fastest passage made by any of the old *Empresses* was the voyage of the *Empress of Japan* from Victoria to Yokohama that commenced on June 26, 1897. Her average speed was 17.144 knots, and her steaming time 10 days 3 hours and 39 minutes. It will be noted that this was a westbound passage, whereas the fastest trans-Pacific voyages have almost invariably been made eastbound, from Yokohama to Race Rocks. The old *Empress of Japan's* best time eastbound was 10 days 10 hours. More recent records are as follows:

June, 1913 — *Empress of Russia* (maiden voyage), Yokohama to Race Rocks, 9 days 5 hours 29 minutes; average speed slightly under 19 knots; Captain Edward Beetham and Chief Engineer James Adamson.

May, 1914 — *Empress of Asia*, Yokohama to Race Rocks, 9 days 2 hours 44 minutes; average speed 19.19 knots; fastest day 20.4 knots; Captain Samuel Robinson and Chief Engineer W.J.P. Davies.

May, 1914 — *Empress of Russia*, Yokohama to Race Rocks, 8 days 18 hours 31 minutes; average speed 19.86 knots; Captain A.W. Davison and Chief Engineer James Adamson.

June, 1923 — *Empress of Canada*, Yokohama to Race Rocks, 8 days 10 hours 53 minutes; average speed 20.6 knots; fastest day 21.2 knots; Captain A.J. Hailey and Chief Engineer James Lamb.

July, 1924 — *Empress of Asia*, Yokohama to Race Rocks, 8 days 14 hours 48 minutes; average speed 20.2 knots; fastest day 20.63 knots; Captain L.D. Douglas and Chief Engineer R.H. Shaw. (This was not a record run, but it was the fastest voyage ever made by either the *Empress of Asia* or the *Empress of Russia*.)

August, 1930 — *Empress of Japan* (maiden voyage), Yokohama to Race Rocks, 8 days 6 hours 27 minutes; average speed 21.04 knots; Captain Samuel Robinson and Chief Engineer James Lamb.

February, 1931 — *Empress of Japan*, Yokohama to Race Rocks, 8 days 3 hours 18 minutes; average speed 21.47 knots; Captain Samuel Robinson and Chief Engineer James Lamb.

April, 1931 — *Empress of Japan*, Yokohama to Race Rocks, 7 days 20 hours 16 minutes; average speed 22.27 knots; Captain Samuel Robinson and Chief Engineer James Lamb. (The fastest passage yet made on this route.)

May, 1931 — *Empress of Canada*, Yokohama to Honolulu, 6 days 11 hours 31 minutes; average speed 21.78 knots (a record run between these ports, and the highest average speed ever maintained by the *Canada*); Honolulu to Race Rocks, 4 days 12 hours 21 minutes; average speed 21.47 knots; Captain A.J. Hailey and Chief Engineer W.H. Froude.

August, 1931 — *Empress of Canada*, Yokohama to Race Rocks, 8 days 2 hours 34 minutes; average speed 21.57 knots; Captain L.D. Douglas and Chief Engineer J.B. Deans. (Fastest passage made by the *Canada* on this route.)

May, 1935 — *Empress of Japan*, Yokohama to Honolulu, 6 days 8 hours 39 minutes, average speed 22.16 knots; Honolulu to Race Rocks, average speed 22.37 knots (the latter being the highest average the *Japan* attained); Captain L.D. Douglas and Chief Engineer R.H. Shaw.

April, 1938 — *Empress of Japan*, Yokohama to Honolulu, 6 days 8 hours 33 minutes; average speed 22.17 knots; Captain L.D. Douglas and Chief Engineer R.H. Shaw.

The date given in each case is the arrival date at Vancouver.

Catalogue of Illustrations

The sources of all illustrations not identified in either their captions or in the index below is the collection of the Vancouver Maritime Museum. If we have inadvertently misattributed sources or overlooked same, we apologize sincerely. A photographic record reaching back over one hundred years and from differing sources does, at times, leave a confusing trail behind it.

Legend: (refers to position of illustration on page)
U. Upper   R. Right   L. Lower   Lt. Left
U.Lt. Upper Left   L.Lt. Lower Left
U.R. Upper Right   L.R. Lower Right

Mrs. A.S. Barker, Jr.	113 inset
British Columbia Archives & Records Service	U.Lt.16
Dr. Wallace B. Chung	1, L.Lt.12, R.12, 21, 24, 33, L.Lt.37, L.R.38, L.40, 55, 56, 68(5,9), L.85, L.R.89, all 109, L.Lt. & centre 120
Mr. Robert Gibson	68(2), 80, 82, 83, L.85, L.R.120
Hawaii State Archives	116
Historical Society of Seattle & King County	L.53
Dr. W. Kaye Lamb	all 65, 86, all 102 & 103, 130
Mr. Derek S. Low	U.120
Maritime Museum of British Columbia	all 108
Miller & Leonard Advertising	114
Museum of History & Industry, Seattle	R.16, U.Lt.53
Port Moody Museum	10
Puget Sound Maritime Historical Society	U.R. & L.R.53
Mr. Robert D. Turner	38, 68(6), 72, 87, L.R. & L.Lt.107, 113
Vancouver City Archives	7, 9, L.Lt.13, 19
Vancouver Public Library, Historical Photographs	17
Washington State Historical Society	52